Turning to God From Idols:
A Biblical Approach to Addictions

By Gregory L. Madison

AWE OF MY LIFE
PUBLICATIONS
AWE IN AWE

Turning to God from Idols: A Biblical Approach to Addictions

Copyright ©2018 by Gregory L. Madison

AWE OF MY LIFE PUBLICATIONS
www.turningtoGodfromidols.com

All Scripture quotations, unless otherwise indicated, are taken from the *Holy Bible: New International Version* ®. Copyright 1973, 1978, 1984 by International Bible Society. Used by permission of Zondervan Publishing House. All right reserved.

Library of Congress Cataloging-in-Publication Data
Madison, Gregory
Turning to God from Idols: A Biblical Approach to Addictions

ISBN- 978-1987632507

Table of Contents

Clean and Sober for the Right Reasons
A Deeper Study of the Word of God on Addictions

The Aim
Sign Posts
The Process of Change
Celebrate Recovery 8 Principles
Reformer Unanimous' Principles

Preface

"Turning to God from Idols" is a study that addresses addictions from a biblical perspective. Although within this writing, the addiction to substances are frequently mentioned, the study is intended to address any and every addiction. "Turning to God from Idols" really concerns anything that we put before the true and living God (by various means). One of the interesting dynamics of addictions is that before we put an idol before God, we *ourselves* are the first idol and then the object. It is then the idol/addiction, which we try to control and use to our advantage, *uses and controls us instead*.

As quiet as it is kept, my approach has been used over and over down through the centuries. But, in an effort to address addictions without the use of the Bible (per se), people have presented many other methods to explain and combat addictions. Some of these methods give out false information mixed with *some* truth. **You need not read this book if you do not want to be all that God has intended for you to be.** Dr. Edward T. Welch says it best in his book titled "Addictions: A Banquet in the Grave". "This might sound strange, but you don't have to turn to the true God to stop your addiction! I'm sure you've met people who kicked addictions without turning to Christ in repentance and faith. You could probably find strategies that are not Christ-centered that would nevertheless keep you away from alcohol for the rest of your life. But God wants more. He wants us to know Him, serve Him, fear Him, and love Him. Somehow, God must be bigger than our own desires- so big that we worship Him alone."

i

Here is my story

As I look back over my life, it is hard to believe that I was 'hooked' on crack for 23 years. During that time, I participated in both Christian and secular programs (at least 14 or 15). The programs included Veteran facilities, Pacific Garden Mission in Chicago, a farm program in Colorado (owned by Denver Rescue Mission), as well as many others. Very early during my struggle with my addiction to crack (and the other addictions that went with it), I sought to discover what the Bible has to say concerning addictions. In 1996, I began a personal study describing the link between addiction and idolatry. This is now a lifetime study of mine.

Although I had begun to find the answers that I needed concerning addictions, I kept going back to using crack. During those 23 years, the longest time that I remained 'clean and sober' was for 17 months (mainly because I lived away from the city, at that time). I lived in many different cities for 7 years, going from one program to another. At other times, I lived on the streets and with friends (on and off drugs). It was in the year of 2003 that I decided that there was no way that I was ever going to quit using drugs again. This was the first time that I had ever stooped to that level.

Since I had made such a decision, I thought that it would be best for me to go to Florida where I could find what is thought to be the purest cocaine in the United States. After spending the winter in Florida and going back north in the summer for two years, I returned to Cleveland, Ohio. God began to convince me, more and more, that His way is best and that my actions were highly offensive towards both He and my fellowman. I thought of how I was not only depriving myself, but also God (as well as others). This led to a decision to remain in Cleveland and seek out the help of my family and the faith community. I vowed never to move away until I had thoroughly allowed God to deal with my addictions and was 'stable'.

For about the next 6 years I went into the VA several times, joined different churches, and continued to read and write Bible-based material on addictions. I, also, attended Bible-based support groups in the city of Cleveland (which I am tremendously grateful for). I would sometimes stay clean for months at a time, only to return to drugs.

In January of 2011 I heard that my grandmother in Memphis, Tennessee was very ill. I knew that I could be of no help to her (or anyone) because of the investments that I was making on my addictions. I started doing everything I needed to do so that I would be able to assist my grandmother and her husband (86 and 96, at the time) as soon as possible. Through the power of Christ, the strength of His word, the prayers and support of my dad, and with the aid of a local church, as well as others, I was able to begin a consistent walk with Christ for 2 months before traveling to Memphis. One year after my first visit to Memphis, I moved there. And so now, the things that are most important to me are hearing God and being used by Him each and every day. True and lasting sobriety, that is pleasing to God, is found in Christ alone.

(to be continued)

Introduction

Over the centuries addictions have been the root of many problems. Addictions have been around since the beginning of time. The addictions of today are vast and powerful. As quiet as it is kept, addiction is just another form of an ancient ritual. This age-old practice is what is known as idolatry. Alcohol, pornography, illicit sex, drugs, gambling… become gods. Before you read this book, I would like for you to know that I do not claim to have all the answers. The Bible does. The Bible *itself* tells us so.

(God) hath given us <u>all things that pertain to life</u> and godliness, through the knowledge of him that hath called us to glory and virtue (Jesus).
2 Peter 1:3

*All scripture is given by inspiration of God, and is <u>**profitable**</u> for doctrine, for reproof, for correction, for instruction in righteousness: <u>That the man of God may be perfect, thoroughly furnished unto all good works</u>.*
2 Timothy 3:16-17

*The law of the LORD is **perfect**, converting the soul: the testimony of the LORD is **sure**, making wise the simple. The statues of the LORD are right, rejoicing the heart: the commandment of the LORD is pure, **enlightening the eyes**. The fear of the LORD is **clean, enduring forever**: the judgments of the LORD are true and righteous altogether. More to be desired are they than gold, yea, than much fine gold: sweeter also than honey and the honeycomb. Moreover by them is thy servant warned: and in keeping of them there is great reward.* ***Psalms 19:7-11***

iv

*For whatsoever things were written aforetime were written for our **learning**, that we through patience and comfort of the **scriptures** <u>**might have hope**</u>.*
Romans 15:4

*Now these things were **our examples**, to the intent we should not lust after evil things, as they also lusted.*
1 Corinthians 10:6

There are many different things to be said concerning addictions that can be drawn right out of the Bible. A really great example is how Isaiah 55 can be applied to addictions. Edward T. Welch asks his readers, **"Do you have a good grasp on the wealth of biblical material that speaks precisely to the modern problems of addictions? Can you go through any book in scripture, even if it doesn't mention alcohol, food, or sex, and see how it speaks to addictions?"** From the very start, I have had a desire to express what the Bible says about addictions. Again, I have devoted my life to this cause.

I am not claiming that this is the one and only way to break free from an addiction. It is encouraging to know that there <u>are</u> many programs available for those who struggle with addictions. Each of the programs has their benefits. Some are more relevant than others. Each of these programs deals with different aspects of addiction (psychological, medical, spiritual…). It is my opinion that **the most important aspect of addiction that must be addressed is the spiritual aspect.** I believe that if people do not address the spiritual issues of addiction (from the very start) then they will always lack the level of sobriety that is necessary in becoming whole.

I am not making any apologies for presenting sobriety as found in Christ. After all, **sobriety in Christ is the highest form of sobriety known to man**. <u>**There has never been anyone as sane and sober as Jesus (nor will there ever be)**</u>. 500 years before Jesus was even born the prophet Isaiah said that, "The Spirit of the LORD will rest on him- the Spirit of wisdom and of understanding, the Spirit of counsel and of power, the Spirit of knowledge and of the fear of the LORD- and he will delight in the fear of the LORD" (Isaiah 11:2-3a). Just what every addict needs!

In an article that is titled "The Distinguishing Feature of Christian Counseling", Dr. Wayne A. Mack says that "Christ-centered counseling involves understanding the nature and courses of our human difficulties, understanding the ways we are unlike Christ in our values, aspirations, desires, thoughts, feelings, choices, attitudes, actions, and responses. Resolving those sin-related difficulties includes being redeemed and justified through Christ, receiving God's forgiveness through Christ, and acquiring from Christ the enabling power to replace unChristlike (sinful) patterns of life with Christlike, godly ones."

The title of "Turning to God from Idols" comes from 1 Thessalonians 1:9, which commended the Thessalonians for "turning to God from idols to serve the living and true God". In his article titled "Idols of the Heart", David Powlinson states that "idolatry is far the most frequently discussed problem in the scriptures". Perhaps, this is because the One who inspired the scriptures knew that idolatry would be an ever-increasing problem. **I am, personally, convinced that <u>if the Word of God had nothing to say about addictions, then God would not have created us</u>**. The purpose of this book is to uncover the identity of addictions, to encourage the reader to continually turn to Christ for answers, and to promote the joy of fellowshipping with the living and true God and with others. <u>If you don't remember anything else, I</u>

want you to remember the underlining principle behind all
that is said.

*The reason that God created us is so that we could have
the highest degree of intimacy/fellowship with Him,
radiating His image and likeness and thereby become a
blessing to others in whatever way He chooses. Addictions
prevent this from happening.*

Here is a piece of a 'Puritan' writing from "The Valley of
Vision" to help explain just what I am saying:

Man's Great End

LORD OF ALL BEING,

There is one thing that deserves my greatest care,
That calls forth my ardent desires,
That is, that I may answer the great end for which
I am made—
To glorify thee who hast given me being,
And to do all the good I can for my fellow men;
Verily, life is not worth having
If it be not improved for this noble purpose.
Yet, Lord, how little is this the thought of mankind!
Most men seem to live for themselves,
Without much or any regard for thy glory,
Or for the good of others;
They earnestly desire and eagerly pursue
The riches, honours, pleasures of this life,
As if they supposed that wealth, greatness,
merriment,

could make their immortal souls happy;
But, alas, what false delusive dreams are these!
And how miserable ere long will those be that
sleep in them,
for all our happiness consists in loving thee,
and being holy as thou art holy.

One other thing that I want to make perfectly clear from the very start is that *I do not believe in the 'disease concept' of addictions*. For years, I struggled with trying to decide if addiction was a disease. I like the way that Mark E. Shaw emphasizes that addicts must get rid of what he calls "a victim mentality" is his book titled "The Heart of Addiction: A Biblical Perspective".

I could go on and on with this point, but I will ask just one question to prove that addiction is not a disease; How and when did you ever see someone repent of a disease?

I beg of you, as an earnest reader, to be patient with me through the first part of "Turning to God from Idols" while I expose the spiritual nature of addictions through reasoning. **It is very important to have a solid foundation from which to develop our sobriety**. I have spent a lot of time explaining the nature, origin, and effects of addiction in order to reveal how severe of a problem we face. Another reason for looking at the true nature of addictions and their origin is to give us a basis for turning to God from idols. The second part is a description of repentance from idolatry. And third and final part of turning to God from idols is found in our rejoicing (delighting) in the true and living God.

I prefer the subtitle "The Foundation of Sanctification", but "A Biblical Approach to Addictions" helps everyone to understand what the writing is about at a glance. The original title of this writing was "Idolatry Assassination" which comes from Genesis 35:2 and Joshua 24:14.

Genesis 35:2 So Jacob said to his household and to all who were with him, "Put away the foreign gods which are among you, and purify yourselves, and change your garments." (NAS)

Joshua 24:14 Now therefore, fear the Lord and serve Him in sincerity and truth; and put away the gods which your fathers served beyond the River and in Egypt and serve the Lord.

Both passages beckon the people to "put away" their idols. This book is designed to guide people through a process of putting idolatry to death. One of the key phrases in Joshua that is instrumental in dealing with idolatry/addictions is "to fear the Lord and serve Him". It is my desire, as well as God's (even more so), that every addict would make the decisions that would allow them to put away the things that stand between them and God (which, also, hinder their growth, their relationships, and their duties). Give unto the LORD the glory due unto his name; worship the LORD in the beauty of holiness (Psalms 29:2).

As I have already stated, "Turning to God from Idols" has three sections. I encourage my readers not to look at these sections as a 'checklist'. (Though I don't *fully* endorse the 12 steps of *Alcoholics Anonymous* I don't believe that *they* should be taken as a 'checklist either**). I believe that a lot of the various 'list/steps' that people come up with all have common features and are more of an *observation* of what God is doing in a person's heart than a 'to do list'.**

For with the heart man believes unto righteousness (Romans 10:10).

Finally, I do not apologize for the great number of bible references. Addiction is such a tremendous foe, it is all too gracious of our Commander and Chief to give us a great and vast arsenal to combat the war that has been waged against the souls of men, women, boys and girls everywhere. **Study hard and study long** to not only experience the freedom that God wants for you, but to be able to pass it on to others as well!

<u>Phase 1</u>

Reason

A. Reasoning (God's reasoning with us)
B. The Reality of Addictions
C. The Reality of Deceit
D. The Real You

Chapter One

A. Reasoning
(God's reasoning with us)
In the beginning was the Word

Just as sure as you have been created in the image of God, you have the ability to reason. God has been reasoning with man from the beginning of creation. Just look at the first three chapters of Genesis! The scriptures tell us how God reasoned with Israel during Isaiah's time.

Come now, and let us reason together, saith the Lord...
Isaiah 1:18a (KJV)

And, there are many other passages that refer to reasoning and understanding which are mentioned in scriptures. Reasoning is one the essential elements of sobriety. In fact, 'cool reasoning' is just one of the definitions of sobriety. (You will find a more extensive definition of sobriety in Appendix B). Reasoning, in turn, gives us understanding. We will discuss understanding later as well.

Where are you?

Logically, (*reasonably, no pun intended*) speaking, I would suppose that the first issue in dealing with an addiction is whether a person, <u>actually</u>, wants to get rid of an addiction. The second thing that the person must ask is <u>why</u> they should put an end to their addiction. If an individual does not see their addiction as being a problem, then it is not likely that they are willing to make any changes. After all, the activity that they are involved with may not be a 'problem' for them (though it may be to those with whom they have their dealings, i.e. relatives, employers, God…). And even if the individual admits that they have a problem; they may not *want* to change. And so, we must ask ourselves, "what's wrong with a particular activity".

The way God sees it

The best thing for us to do is to ask God to search us. I can guarantee that if you are really serious, that He will do just that!

Psalms 139:23-24 says, ***Search me, O God, and know my heart: try me, and know my thoughts: And see if there be any wicked way in me, and lead me in the way everlasting.***

I love a good chess game. After 43 years of sporadic playing, I have recently discovered that if you develop a discipline of good 'posture', then you don't have to worry so much about being 'overtaken' by your opponent. And it is this same 'posture' that can set you up for victory, also (though you may not have 'intentionally' began to attack). This 'posture' (if you will) is like a 'default mode'. I believe that the 'posture' that God has given us of being open before Him proves to be a 'default mode' for our protection against addictions (or any other evil), and to be victorious in our walk with Him. Perhaps, this is, at least, part of what Solomon meant in Proverbs 2:10-11 when he said that, "when wisdom enters your heart, and knowledge is pleasant to your soul, discretion will preserve you; understanding will keep you". I cannot always tell you what the best move is in a chess game. But, I can tell you that the best move (perhaps, the first move) to make in dealing with addictions is to ask God to search you on a regular basis!

The goal

It is important for us to see that the goal that God has for us is bigger than *just* a life that is free of addiction. Proverbs 29:18 says that where there is no vision the people perish. **What the Lord God desires most is our intimacy. Just as you are, perhaps, intimately involved with an addiction (in some cases, intricately and extensively). God wants that the same intimacy for Himself.** Here are just a few questions to help you with this:

1. Am I just as amazed with Jesus as I am towards that which I am addicted to (or even more)?
2. Do I hunger for God as much (even more) than I do other things?
3. What is my attitude towards God before, during, and after being involved in addiction?
4. Do I embrace the presence of God as much or more as I do anything else?

And speaking of vision; here is one that is laid before us by Dr. Edward T. Welch;

"Imagine having drug cravings subdued by the joy of knowing and obeying Christ. Imagine having temptations lose their allure because there is more pleasure in walking humbly with our God. Imagine waking up and strategizing how to please the God who loves you rather than where you will get your next drink."

Before the Lord

It is at this point that I must pause and ask you if you have ever started a relationship with Jesus Christ. Jesus said that He is the way, the truth, and the life and that no man comes to the Father but through Him (John 14:6). **The most sobering thing, in all the world is to go before God. And so, the question is; Where do you stand before God? To be before God is not only sobering, but for us who put our trust in Christ it is comforting. To stand before God with a clear conscious is one of the greatest strengths there is in dealing with an addiction.** I cannot overemphasize that intimacy with God is one of the major themes of this book. Have you called upon Him to cleanse you of your sins? **Don't fool yourself, <u>apart from the blood of Christ you don't even have a connection with God!</u>**

Behold, the LORD's hand is not shortened, that it cannot save; neither His ear heavy, that it cannot hear; But your iniquities have separated between you and your God, and your sins have hidden His face from you, that He will not hear.
Isaiah 59:1-2

Why do you want to quit?

Now, back to our reasoning. Some of the other questions you must ask yourself are; Do you want to be free from your addiction or just the consequences? For how long? At what price? For what reason? How bad do you want sobriety? How much effort are you willing to put in?

And so, here's the question once again: Why do you want to end your addiction? This is where your motivation lies.

Without motivation, there is no hope. **There are four basic reasons why a person decides to abstain from an addiction. (Only four, although they sometimes coincide with one another or can be expressed in other words).**

1. **To better their lives**
2. **To avoid the consequences**
3. **To better the lives of those around them**
4. **Out of reverence for God**

A frame of reverence

That last answer is *the* most important element in turning from bad habits and developing and maintaining healthy habits that honor God. In fact, it is *the* answer to addictions as set forth in scripture. Our reverence for God is related to the intimacy that we have with Him. Reverence for God is essential to life, society, mankind...

The world is governed by laws (laws and principles). **Among the greatest principles of life; the *fear of the Lord* is <u>completely</u> indispensable.** Solomon, a man who experienced much of what the world has to offer, said to be the wisest man who ever lived, the wealthiest as well, emphasized the importance of reverencing God in Eccles. 12: 13.

> *Now all has been heard; here is the conclusion of the matter: Fear God and keep his commandments, for this is the whole duty of man.*

Because Solomon knew a lot about life, he knew that we cannot do without the fear of the Lord. **Where there is no reverence for God there is only calamity, confusion and**

disorder. Irreverence for God is devoid of the blessing of God. Where there is no reverence for God there is no wisdom, because wisdom *comes from God*. Irreverence leaves us vulnerable to deception because **in rejecting God we reject the truth**. <u>Entire nations have been destroyed because of their irreverence for God</u>. Untold lives have been ruined because of this same hideous disposition. James 3:15-16 gives us a clue of where irreverence towards the Creator leads. Verse 15 says:

> *This wisdom is not that which comes down from above, but is earthly, natural, demonic. For where jealousy and selfish ambition exist, there is disorder and every evil thing.*

The fear of the Lord (or reverence for God) is an acknowledgment of His presence, His love, His wisdom and His ownership. Vine's Expository Dictionary of Biblical Words says that reverence is "the recognition of the power and position of an individual and render Him proper respect". The **Thorndike-Barnhart Comprehensive Dictionary says that to revere means to love and respect deeply, honor greatly and show reverence for.**

The Lord told Samuel that those who honor Him, He will also honor (1 Sam. 2:30). Other rewards for revering God are harmony (Lev. 25:36), preservation (Deut. 6:24), confidence (Prov.14:26), and ease (Ps. 25:12-13). There are of course, many other rewards for revering the Lord; these are just a few of the blessings that show how the fear of the Lord is connected to our <u>mental</u> state of being. The rewards of reverencing God are beyond compare.

On the other hand, wherever there is a lack of reverence, a disregard for the Almighty, the consequences are just the opposite of the rewards for reverencing God. **Whereas our** reverence produces harmony, irreverence produces *disharmony*. Irreverence *prevents* prosperity. *Dis-ease* is the outcome of irreverence. Instead of deliverance, irreverence for God leads to bondage. Discontent is closely related to irreverence. Folly is, also, a trademark of an irreverent disposition. Irreverence for God ultimately leads to death. How can we leave out the Lord and expect <u>anything</u> good to occur? All that *is* good comes from God. This is just a brief account of some of the consequences of irreverence.

The scriptures give an account of people who refused to revere and honor God. Among them are Pharaoh and his servants, Amalek and backslidden Israel. In each situation, their irreverence led to disaster. <u>Irreverence is a choice that people make</u>. Proverbs 1:29 says that the simple ones, scorners, fools and those who hated knowledge did not <u>choose</u> the fear of the Lord. Jeremiah 44:10 equates irreverence with a lack of humility. **<u>Behind every sin is the element of irreverence.</u>** Jeremiah 2:19 describes irreverence for God as an evil thing. Zephaniah 3:7 explains how those who refuse to revere the Lord were corrupt in all their doings. Because of their lack of reverence Israel played the harlot against God (Jer. 3:8). They honored God with their lips, but their heart was far from Him (Matt. 15:8). The priests who lacked reverence despised His name (Mal. 1:6).

The consequences for irreverence are severe. The word of the Lord warns us of some of the *specific* consequences that are the result of irreverence and disregard for God. We see that Amalek was blotted out because of their irreverence for the Lord (Duet. 25:17-19). The people in 2 Kings 17:35 were slain by lions because of their lack of reverence. Ps. 55:19 says that God will afflict the irreverent. Other consequences specifically mentioned;

Their years will be shortened   Pro. 10:27

It will not be well with them	Eccl. 8:13
His days are as a shadow	Eccl. 8:13
Punishment	Zep. 3:7

Irreverence for God leads only to calamity and confusion. Without God there is no order, no direction. Those who make the choice of ignoring, slighting and despising the Lord are placing themselves in a precarious situation. They are disregarding a primarily essential element of life, a governing law within the universe. **A refusal to revere God is both irrational and insane.**

I cannot overemphasize the issue of reverence. It is for this reason that I have devoted a special section to the fear of the Lord (found in Appendix D). In his "Treatise on the Fear of God", John Bunyan calls the fear of the Lord the highest duty, "because it is, as I may call it, not only a duty in itself, but, as it were, the salt that seasoneth every duty. For there is no duty performed by us that can by any means be accepted by God, if it be not seasoned with godly fear."

Resolved

When God reasons with us we get a view of reality. With a proper reverence for God we are able to see the reality of addictions. Be sure that you reverently build your foundation of sobriety on the reasoning that God has given in His word, by His Holy Spirit! Do you remember how I said at the beginning of this chapter how reasoning requires understanding? It is for this reason that the Lord has led me to construct an outline on understanding. Before you go any further in your reading, I need for you to read the section on "Understanding" in Appendix A! Go to Appendix B and read "What is Addiction/idolatry?", "A Deeper Study of the Word of God Addictions", and "The Importance of Using Various Resources", as well, before continuing to the next chapter!

Chapter Two
A. The Reality of Addiction: Idolatry
Addictions dishonor God

Our quest for sobriety <u>must</u> begin by addressing and exposing addictions at the core of their being. As God reasons with us, we are exposed to reality. In order for any type of lasting change to take place, a person must be *convinced* that what they are doing is wrong. And so, change begins with conviction. Conviction is defined as **a settled persuasion**, the state of being **convinced**. Unless we are thoroughly convinced that our actions are wrong, we have no reason to change.

Conviction is based on reasoning. Again, one of the remarkable things about God is His ability and willingness to reason with us as He did with Israel.

Come now, let us <u>reason</u> together, says the Lord; though
your sins be as scarlet, they shall be
white as snow; though they be red as crimson,
they shall be as wool.
Isaiah 1:18, emphasis mine

Conviction

In his book called "Addictions: A Banquet in the Grave", Dr. Ed Welch says that "one way that God loves His people is by sending His Spirit to "convict the world of guilt in regard to sin" (Jn. 16:8). This is not condemnation; it is God's way of rescuing us. Sin is a path that leads to tragedy

11

and despair. If someone saw you on such a path and did nothing, that would be unloving. But the Spirit of God awakens our hearts to the presence of sin in our lives, and then convinces us that He forgives sin because of Jesus Christ and gives us peace. It is when we experience no conviction of sin that we should be most alarmed."

In his most famous devotional that is titled, "My Utmost for His Highest", Oswald Chambers says, "conviction of sin is one of the rarest things that ever strikes a man.
It is the threshold of an understanding of God. Jesus Christ said that when the Holy Spirit came He would convict of sin, and when the Holy Spirit rouses a man's conscience and brings him into the presence of God, it is not his relationship with men that bothers him, but his relationship with God— 'against thee, Thee only, have I sinned, and done this evil in Thy sight'." (Ps. 51:4a.)

In his book, "How to Help People Change", Jay Adams states that, "In convicting us of sin, God is calling on us to recognize that the change we must make is not simply good advice, it is an imperative. He is telling us that what we have done is not merely inconvenient, counterproductive, or undesirable, it is flat wrong and *must* be changed."
"Moreover, by requiring conviction, God is saying that He cares about us. Unlike the father who lets his child's disobedience slip by unmentioned, God shows concern enough to convict, to go to the trouble of arguing the case and convincing us of our wrong. Why? Because He cares about the fellowship He sustains with His children. He knows that sin breaks of that fellowship. He wants fellowship to remain intact or, where conviction is necessary, to be restored."

Assets and liabilities of various addictions

So, what must be done in order to convince someone that an addiction is dishonoring to God? After all, anyone who has been deeply involved with the love of an addiction is *readily* willing and able to offer a pretty good defense of his or her addiction's <u>usefulness</u>. Personally, I must confess that my own pursuit of an intimate relationship with crack cocaine for 23 years (off and on) was not just so that I would wind up homeless, single, childless, and without a future outside of the grace of God. I really thought that the drugs were 'doing something' for me.

Dr. Welch offers a list of *perceived* (or at best temporary) assets. He says that, "even with all the associated misery, people drink because on some level drinking does something for them". Their drinking is purposeful.
It may allow a brief opportunity to:

- Forget
- Punish
- Cure self-consciousness and timidity
- Avoid pain
- Fill holes in one's image
- Manage emotions
- Fit in with others
- Prove to yourself that you can do what you want
- Keep loneliness at bay

On the contrary, here are some of the liabilities of addiction. (my own observations)

1.   It is a form of idolatry

2. Poor use of energy
3. Waste of time
4. Waste of money
5. Endangers your health
6. Endangers your safety
7. Endangers the safety of others
8. Non-productive
9. Tears relationships apart
10. Bad example to others
11. Improper use of God's creation
12. Supports those who supply others with harmful sources of addiction
13. Reinforces a false sense of security
14. A stumbling block to others
15. It gives a bad testimony

Ralph O. Burns states that there are five basic questions, which we do well to ask of each and every decision we make.

1. Does it glorify God?
2. Is this thing a weight?
3. Is it becoming a habit?
4. Is this thing a stumbling block to others?
5. Is it a wise thing to do?

Grounds for removal

There are two basic reasons why addictions are wrong. The first reason that addictions are wrong is covered within the remainder of this chapter. The second will be discussed in the next chapter.

a.   Addictions are a form of idol worship.

b. **Addictions are a wasteful thing/they are futile.**

This is another way of stating the reasons for abstaining mentioned in the last chapter, which are;

1. To better our lives
2. To avoid the consequences
3. To better the lives of those around us
4. Out of reverence for God

In "How to Help People Change", Jay Adams says,

> "But why is conviction so important? Because it pertains to the counselee's relationship to God. **Much change that is offered today in counseling— even in the Name of Christ—is sub-Christian. Aimed at little more than making counselees happier, it neglects the basic reason why a believer must change to please God. As if God's glory were of secondary importance, His Name's sake is omitted from the picture, out of deference to better health or a more smoothly running marriage. Such considerations, not wrong in themselves, are quite wrong when they are not subordinated to the greater purpose of pleasing and honoring God."**

Spiritual implications

So, as strange as it may sound, addiction is a form of idolatry. Idolatry is defined as the worship of something created as oppose to the worship of the Creator Himself. An idol is something of human manufacture, which people have substituted for the true and living God- anything that stands between us and God or something we substitute for God. **Worship was originally spelled "worthship" and it means to acknowledge the worth of the object worshipped. Can it be that drugs, alcohol or something else is worth more to us than God?** This is what idolatry is.

Little children, keep yourselves from idols (false gods) – [from anything that would occupy the place in your heart owed to God, from any sort of substitute for Him that would take first place in your life.]
1 John 5:21 (Amplified version)

Is there anything that you have allowed to take God's place? Anything? Ed Welch has stated that idolatry is "anything on which we set our affections and indulge as an excessive and sinful attachment. Idolatry includes anything we worship: the lust for pleasure, respect, love, power, control, or freedom from pain".

There are at least four ways that we worship:

1. **Through making sacrifices**
2. **Allowing something to dominate or control**
3. **Give honor/glorify, praise**
4. **To exhibit trust**

Making sacrifices

First, people allow an addiction to take God's place by making sacrifices for it. People sacrifice possessions for drugs, alcohol and other addictions (sacrificing houses, cars, land, jewelry, furniture, etc.). People often buy things and later sell them for a much lesser value in order to supply their habits. Many individuals will forfeit the opportunity to purchase a home or a car...because they would rather spend money on an addiction. People sacrifice their bodies (in various ways). The scripture teaches that God wants us to sacrifice our bodies to Him.

I beseech you therefore, brethren, by the mercies of God, that ye present your bodies as a living sacrifice, holy acceptable unto God, which is your reasonable service.
Romans 12:1 (KJV)

Many of us have sacrificed relationships on behalf of our involvement with an addiction. There are people who devote their lives to an addiction, just as others devote their lives to God. Unfortunately, some people actually die because of their addiction. **The ultimate sacrifice is to disregard the love of God, reject a relationship with Him and go to hell!**

The sacrifices that people have made towards addictions, down through the ages cannot be numbered. Who knows how much money could have been put to good use? Who knows how many lives could have been saved? Only God knows of all the time and energy, as well as resources, that could have been sacrificed for things that give glory to God and aid to humanity.

Dominated by an addiction

Another way that addictions take God's place is when people allow addictions to have dominion (or control). This is what it means to be "under the influence." It is to be ruled by something or someone. "People are ruled by plants", a friend once said. I didn't understand what he was saying until he explained that there are some who allow the substances which drugs and alcohol come from to dictate their actions.

According to the scriptures, this is completely opposite from what God intends. Psalm 104:14 says, "He causeth the grass to grow for the cattle, and herb for the service of man." When God created man and woman, He blessed them and said for them to "subdue" the earth (Genesis 1:28). To subdue means to bring into subjection. So, rather than being dominated by the things He has created, God wants us to dominate them. The irony of it all is that God created everything for His glory and to be useful to mankind.

God does not want us to love the things of this world (see 1 John 2:15). Our deepest devotion should belong to God. Jesus said that the greatest commandment is to "love the Lord God with all our heart, our soul, and our mind" (Matthew 22:37). God alone deserves our allegiance. God alone should control us.

Glory, honor and praise

People, also, allow addictions to take God's place by glorifying them. How many people claim that they could not make it through the day without their gin? Or, they brag about the great high they get from heroin? People rant and rave on street corners about how good the crack is from this or that dealer. And then, there are the TV commercials and billboards that render undeserved praise and glory to alcoholic beverages. Just look at how gambling and pornography is being glorified and promoted! Do these same people promote Jesus Christ (the way, the truth, and the life)? Absolutely not!

The fact is that addictions should be disdained, because of all the destruction they have caused. And then, people have a way of idolizing addictions to the point that all their thoughts are centered upon them. The addiction becomes the most valuable thing to them. The response to this from the scriptures tells us to give to the Lord the glory that is due His name (Ps. 29:2).

A love/trust relationship

Yet another way that we express the worth of an addiction is by the trust that we put in it. Just as some people see God as being trust-worthy, others believe that a particular addiction is worthy of their trust. By using it for some advantage (to boost our ego, relieve stress, loosen our inhibitions, etc.) we are stating that it is trust-worthy. As I mentioned before, the addict looks to their addiction to serve a particular purpose. A friend of mine defines addiction as a pathological love/trust relationship between an individual and a mind or mood-altering substance.

The idols in the Bible vs. the idols of today

There are many similarities between the way idols affected Biblical characters and how addictions affect people today. 2 Chronicles 28:23 gives us one example. The verse records how King Ahaz "sought help from idols." People seek all kinds of help from addictions. As was already mentioned, people look for courage, rejuvenation, and a number of other things in an addiction. The verse goes onto say that the idols were the ruin of King Ahaz and all of Israel.

Addictions have been the ruin of many. Ahaz should have sought help from the Lord, as those who look to addictions should.

Those in Thessalonica during the Apostle Paul's ministry were said to have repented by turning to God from idols to serve the living and true God. False gods just don't stack up to the living and true God.

Answering to God

Andrew Comiskey says that some who struggle with an addiction to homosexual behavior "live in a time when many voices within the church are proclaiming other "gospels," other ways of being "saved."

> **"These voices invariably center on man's needs and have nothing to say about a holy God, one whose very holiness, when we come into His presence, starts the process of healing and redemption in our souls. Instead of being taught to look up and worship, we're focused on our problem."**

Ed Welch says that addicts "have no awareness that what they are doing has anything to do with God. The problem, they believe, is simply within themselves. It is neither against God nor others. It is one thing to acknowledge that we occasionally do wrong: it is something else to acknowledge that what we did was sin- it was against God"
.

Marks of idolatry

Now, let's look at some of the phrases that describe Israel's addiction to idols from the scriptures. See if you can recognize any of the similarities that these phrases have with the addictions of today!

1. they went a whoring after other gods
    Ex. 34:15
2. they corrupted themselves   Deut. 32:5
3. unmindful of the Rock that
    begat them   v.18
4. did evil in the sight of the Lord
    Judges 2:11
5. not mindful of God's wonders
    Neh. 9:16
6. rebelled against God   v.26
7. cast God's law behind their back   v.26
8. thought their way was hidden from God
    Isa. 40:27
9. shame, fear, hunger   44:9,10
10. a deceived heart has turned him aside
    v.20
11. cannot see that he is holding fast to a lie
    v.20
12. walked after their own vanity
    Jer. 2:5
13. after things that do not profit   2:8
14. My fear is not in thee
    2:19
15. forgot the Lord days without number
    2:32
16. covered with confusion   3:25
17. destruction upon destruction   4:20

18.	they have no understanding	v.22
19.	refuse to receive correction	5:3
20.	they made their faces harder than a rock	v.3
21.	did not tremble at God's presence	v.22
22.	they had no delight in the word of the Lord	6:10
23.	after other gods to their harm	7:6
24.	they hold fast to deceit	8:5
25.	no peace, no health, trouble	v.15
26.	they proceed from evil to evil	9:3
27.	they are not valiant for the truth	v.3
28.	weary themselves to commit iniquity	v.5

What about you?

Can you see how these various phrases relate to addictions? Are you guilty of the same attitudes and actions? Personally, I am forever grateful that the Lord has forgiven me of all the times that I chose to encompass my life with idolatry. **This is by no means a complete list on the marks of idolatry. In my studies on idolatry I have found that the phrases of this nature could conservatively be stretched to six to eight hundred phrases that refer to the expressions of idolatry.** Please take the time to study the outline of idolatry in Appendix C as well! The goal is that we start developing a godly sorrow over our attitudes and actions related to addictions. <u>This is an element of sobriety that you will find to be indispensable!</u>

Godly sorrow brings repentance that leads to salvation and leaves no regret, but worldly sorrow brings death.
2 Corinthians 7:10

I cannot overemphasize the importance of seeing addictions as idols, and therefore irreverent towards God. These are the spiritual implications of addictions. In the next chapter, we will look at how impractical addictions are. In today's world people are inclined to use the impracticality of addictions as a starting point and pass over the spiritual implications (or they may imply that the practical implications are spiritual in and of themselves). But, the fact that addictions are an offence to God must be deeply considered before we go on to looking at how impractical addictions are.

Chapter Three
C. The Reality of Deceit
Addictions have no lasting value

In the previous chapter, we exposed how addiction is wrong because it is an act of false worship (which is an insult to God). By the same token, people disrespect themselves and others by relishing addictions. The very *nature* of idolatry is impractical. One of the definitions for an idol comes from the New Unger's Bible Dictionary. **An idol is "an empty thing, rendered elsewhere 'trouble,' 'iniquity,' 'vanity,' 'wickedness,' etc. The primary idea of the root word seems to be emptiness, nothingness, as a breath or a vapor. The Hebrew word for idol (awen) denotes a vain, false, wicked thing and expresses at once the essential nature of idols and the consequences of their worth." Just like idols, addictions have an emptiness about them.**

Scriptural Proof

Over and over the scriptures warn us of the dangers of being involved with things that are not of God or opposed to the will of God. Idolatry is listed among the works of the flesh in Gal. 5:19-21. Galatians 6:8 says that those who sow to their flesh will "of the flesh reap corruption". The scriptures give us clear warning that idols are empty and troublesome. Note the emphasis that I have placed on certain words and phrases!

Their <u>sorrows shall be multiplied</u> who hasten after another god...

24

Psalm 16:4a

They shall be turned back and utterly <u>put to shame</u>, who trust in idols, who say to molten images, "You are our gods."
Isaiah 42:17 (NAS)

I can remember the disappointment connected to my crack addiction. Though I would sometimes buy large quantities of crack, I would always be disappointed by my desire for more and more.

<u>Confounded</u> *are all that serve graven images, that boast themselves of idols.*
Psalm 97:7

You boast, "We have <u>entered into a covenant with death</u>, with the grave we have made an agreement. When a overwhelming scourge sweeps by, it cannot touch us, for we have <u>made a lie our refuge and falsehood our hiding place</u>.
Isaiah 28:15

Behold, they are all vanity; their works are nothing: their molten images are <u>wind and confusion</u>.
Isaiah 41:29

He <u>feedeth on ashes</u>: a <u>deceived heart</u> hath turned him aside, that he cannot deliver his soul, nor say, Is there not <u>a lie</u> in my right hand?
Isaiah 44:20

25

Every man is brutish in his knowledge: every founder is <u>confounded</u> *by the graven image: for his molten image is* <u>falsehood</u>, *and there is no breath in them.*
Jeremiah 10:14

These are only a few passages that refer to the impotency of idols, of their uselessness and waste. Be sure that you read the Bible for yourself to discover more passages that deal with the dangers of idolatry. (Again, I have provided an outline with some key verses on idolatry in Appendix C worth meditating over).

The high price of idolatry

The Lord told Israel that if they turned from Him and followed idols there would be severe consequences just as there are severe consequences behind the idolatry of addictions. Let's look at the Amplified Version of 1 Kings 9:6-9as an example;

*But if you turn away from following me, you or your children, and will not keep my commandments and statues which I have set before you, but go and serve other gods and worship them, then **I will cut off Israel from the land I have given them**, and this house I have hallowed for my name (renown) I will cast from my sight. And **Israel shall be a proverb and a byword** among all the peoples. **This house shall become a heap of ruins**; every passerby shall be astonished and hiss (with surprise) and say, why has the Lord done thus to this land and to this house?*

Many of the consequences for *Israel's* idolatry are the same that are derived from the idolatry of addictions. *Addicts* often become "cut off from their land" (become homeless).

Addicts become a proverb and a byword (one who is ridiculed, misunderstood, or an outcast).

Sold out

Psalm 106:39 tells how Israel went "a-whoring with their inventions" (idols). They prostituted themselves for idols in a spiritual sense. Idolatry is sometimes referred to as spiritual adultery. In the pursuit of maintaining an addiction people are known to prostitute themselves in many ways. Most people will agree that what they get in return is not worth the price that is paid. Addictions carry a very heavy price, giving nothing in return—besides grief and, at best, a false sense of security (in the long run).

An unequal exchange

From Isaiah 44:9-15, 20, we note the price of idolatry and what it gives in return.

All who make graven idols are **confusion, chaos, and worthlessness**. Their objects [idols] in which they delight **do not profit** them, and their own witnesses [worshipers] do not see or know, so that **they are put to shame**. Who is [such a fool as] to fashion a god or cast a graven image that is **profitable for nothing**? Behold, all his fellows **shall be put to shame**, and the craftsmen, [how can they make a god?] are but men. Let them all be gathered together, let them stand forth, **they shall be terrified**, they shall be **put to shame** together. The iron smith sharpens and uses a chisel and **works** it over the coals; he shapes [the core of the idol] with hammers and forges it with his strong arm. He _**becomes**_ _**hungry**_ and _**his strength fails**_; _**he drinks no water and is**_ _**faint**_. The carpenter stretches out a line, he marks it out with a pencil or red ocher; he fashions [an idol] with planes and marks it out with the compasses; and shapes it to the figure of a man, with the beauty of a man, that it may dwell in a house. He hews for himself cedars and takes the cypress tree or the oak, and lets them grow strong for himself among the trees of the forest; he plants a fir tree or an ash, and the rain nourishes it. Then it becomes fuel for a man to burn, a part of it he takes and warms himself, yes, he kindles a fire and bakes bread, [then out of the reminder, the leavings] he also makes a god and worships it! He [with his own hands [makes it into a graven image and falls down and worships it! That kind of man _**feeds on ashes [and finds his satisfaction in**_ _**ashes**_]! _**A deluded mind has led him astray**_, so that he cannot release and save himself, or ask, is not [this thing I am holding] in my right hand a lie? (Amplified version)

Notice, though much was invested in idols, they proved to be of no practical value.

The futility of addictions

The comments below are from various authors that pertain to the futility or uselessness of addictions.

...we want these substances or activities to give us what we want: good feelings, a better self-image, a sense of power, or whatever our heart is craving. Idols, however, do not cooperate. Rather than mastering our idols, we become enslaved by them

and begin to look like them. How can these lifeless idols exert such power? They dominate because of a quiet presence that hides behind every idol. Satan himself.
Addictions: A Banquet in the Grave, Dr. Edward T. Welch

Liberty comes through law, not apart from it. When is a train most free? Is it when it goes bouncing across the field off the track? No. It is free only when it is confined (if you will) to the track. Then it turns smoothly and efficiently, because that was the way that its maker intended for it to run. It needs to be on the track, structured by the track, to run properly. You too need to be on the track. God's track is found in God's Word.
Godliness through Discipline, Jay Adams

Men are in a restless pursuit after satisfaction in earthly things. They will exhaust themselves in the deceitful delights of sin, and, finding them all to be vanity and emptiness, they will become very perplexed and disappointed. But they will continue their fruitless search. Though wearied, they still stagger forward under the influence of spiritual madness, and though there is no result to be reached except that of everlasting disappointment, yet they press forward. They have no forethought for their eternal state; the present hour absorbs them. They turn to another and another of earth's broken cisterns, hoping to find water where not a drop was ever discovered yet.
Spurgeon

Pornography, in its essential allurement, promises to quench our thirst. In other words, it promises satisfaction. And honestly, it does satisfy—but only for a time. Pretty soon we discover that we are "thirsty" again, and as the years go by we find that we are really never genuinely satisfied. Right? That is because sin never truly satisfies! It does not fulfill us; it depletes us... I thought if I could just see that perfect picture, or have that perfect sexual experience, my life would be full and satisfied. This is the nature of sin.

Pure Freedom, Mike Cleveland

Drunkenness also interferes with our God-given task of subduing the earth. Drunkenness leads to dereliction of duty in the marketplace. Industrial accidents, lateness, and absenteeism are commonplace for the heavy drinker. Unemployment is too familiar. As Proverbs indicates, the norm for drunkenness is poverty (21:17, 23:21). Relationships are disrupted too. "Wine is a mocker, and beer is a brawler" (Prov.20:1). All heavy drinkers leave a wake of broken relationships and victims. In fact, students of alcohol abuse estimate that each heavy drinker leaves a wake of pain for at least ten people. The pain does not always come by way of fistfights, but through car accidents, harsh words, neglect, broken promises, and unwise decisions. Heavy drinkers inevitable hurt others deeply.

Addictions: A Banquet in the Grave, Welch

King Heroin is my shepherd; I shall always want. It maketh me to lie down in gutters: it leadeth me beside troubled waters. It destroyeth my soul: it leadeth me in the paths of wickedness for its own sake. Yea, I shall walk through the valley of poverty and will fear all evil: for thou, Heroin, art with me; thy needle and thy capsule try to comfort me. Thou strippest the table of groceries in the presence of my family: thou robbest my head of reason; my cup runneth over with sorrow. Surely heroin addiction shall stalk me all the days of my life and I will dwell in the house of the damned for ever.

From an unknown source

How families are affected

Addictions prove to be a danger to others as well as to ourselves. Many families suffer because of one family member's addiction. And the problems escalate if there is more than one family member with an addiction. The scriptures give examples of how *idolatry* harmed families during Biblical days.

They mingled with the nations and learned their practices and served their idols, which became a snare to them. They even <u>sacrificed their sons and their daughters to demons and shed innocent blood, the blood of their sons and their daughters, whom they sacrificed to the idols of Canaan</u>; and the land was polluted with the blood. Thus, they became unclean in their practices and played the harlot in their deeds.

Psalm 106:35-39

31

So, they left all the commandments of the Lord their God, made for themselves a molded image and two calves, made a wooded image and worshiped all the host of heaven, and served Baal. And they <u>caused their sons and daughters to pass through the fire</u>, practiced witchcraft and soothsaying, and sold themselves to do evil in the sight of the Lord, to provoke Him to anger.
2 Kings 17:17 (NKJV)

Besides having their lives endangered because of someone's addiction, families may become malnourished, when relying on the money that one or more of its members uses to supply their habit. Families may, also, suffer educationally, emotionally, socially and spiritually because of one or more of its member's addiction/idolatry.

The health hazards of substance abuse

Substance abuse can be impractical due to health reasons. The following is a list of physical conditions that are connected to different substances:

Alcohol: Impairs judgement, distorts vision; causes vitamin deficiencies, stomach ailments, liver damage, and heart problems.

Methamphetamines: Increase heart rate and blood pressure, cause respiratory and cardiovascular problems, hypothermia, convulsions, and damage blood vessels in the brain (causing strokes).

Cigarettes: Cause gastric ulcers, chronic bronchitis, emphysema, heart disease, strokes, and cancer of the mouth, larynx, pharynx, esophagus, lungs, pancreas, cervix, uterus, and bladder.

Cocaine and Crack Cocaine: Cause heart attacks, strokes, and respiratory failure and brain seizures.

Inhalants: Sudden death, suffocation; impair liver, lung, kidneys; cause irreversible brain damage and hepatitis.

Hallucinogens: Cause depression, anxiety, tremors, sleeplessness, lack of coordination, decreased awareness of touch and pain (which can result in self-inflicted injuries), convulsions, coma, and heart and lung failure.

Deep dark deceit

Up until now we have only discussed the <u>nature</u> of addictions/idolatry. "Idols define good and evil in ways contrary to God's definitions. They establish a focus of control that is earth-bound: either in objects (e.g., lust for money), other people ("I need to please my critical father"), or myself (e.g., self-trusting pursuit of my personal agenda)."[1] Such false gods create false laws, false definitions of success and failure, of value and stigma. The origin of addiction paints an even darker picture. **If you are trying to overcome an addiction, give some serious consideration to what you are battling. "Is your method of waging war against your addiction pretty tame? If so, it is because you think you are fighting with a friend. You don't have the heart for it. Are you afraid to fight the way Jesus teaches you for fear that you will no longer have addictions as an insurance policy?"** (Welch)

As you may have guessed, *the prince of darkness* plays a major part in addiction with his ability to lie and deceive. And then, there are *other people* in this world who try to deceive us into turning to idols. But, you might just be surprised over the source of the third party of deception.

Master of deception

Peter encourages followers of Christ to be sober, to be vigilant "because your adversary the devil, as a roaring lion, walks about seeking who he may devour" (1 Pet. 5:8). I hope and pray that you have started a relationship with Christ. Without Jesus, you will not be able to recognize the lies of the devil. This is the one of whom it is said that he is "transformed into an angel of light" (2 Cor. 11:14).

In a book from 1642 called "The Wiles of Satan" William Spurstowe says that Satan "captivates more by his hidden snares than he wounds by his fiery darts. He poisons more as a hissing serpent than he devours as a roaring lion. He cheats more as a tempter than he hurts as an accuser. And as he in his immediate workings has always been (and still is) more

34

mischievous to the church and truth of God by his machinations and arts than by his open force...carried on their designs by fraud and subtlety rather than by a hostile war and defiance". Satan deceives people into satisfying their desires through ungodly means. As quiet as it is kept, Satan wants us all to be just like him so that we will <u>not</u> reflect God's glory.

A world of deception

As I mentioned earlier, there are other people who want to deceive you. 2 Peter 2:18-19 talks about people who entice others by fleshly desires, by sensuality, promising freedom while they themselves are slaves of corruption. Woe unto them that call evil good and good evil, that put darkness for light and light for darkness, that put bitter for sweet and sweet for bitter! Woe unto them that are wise in their own eyes and prudent in their own sight! (Isaiah 5:20-21). These are the type of people who promote addictions.

A heart of deception

Satan as well as others try to deceive us into bowing down to idols. The scriptures talk of *deceitful* lusts (Eph.4:22). Matthew 13:22 refers to *deceitful* riches. The *deceitfulness* of sin is mentioned in Hebrews 3:13. But, right now we are going to consider the one of the agents of deception that must to be given very special attention. This agent of deception is very dear to us all. **This is the greatest enemy we have when left unchecked.**

You may think that Satan is your worst enemy, but according to William Spurstowe,

> "Satan only by moral persuasions, which may be powerful to solicit, but not to constrain... And in this respect, he is (as Jerome truly calls him) a feeble and weak enemy, **who can only overcome him who yields, not him who resists; and hurts him who puts his weapons into his hand, not him who keeps them in his own**".

Jeremiah 17:9 tells us that the heart is deceitful above all things, and it is exceedingly perverse and corrupt and severely, mortally sick! Who can know [perceive, understand, be acquainted with] his own heart and mind? (Amplified version).

Although the book of Psalms was written long before Jeremiah, I think that the Psalmist would have agreed with Jeremiah about the condition of the heart left unto itself. It is no wonder that the Psalmist prayed for the Lord God to search him and know his heart, try him and know his ways and see if there was any wicked way in him and to lead him... (Ps. 139:23-24). The Psalmist also prayed to God to let the words of his mouth and the meditation of his heart to be acceptable in God's sight 19:14

Proverbs 4:23 says to "keep your heart with all diligence, for out of it are the issues of life". We must guard our hearts from idolatry. This leads us right into our next chapter, which addresses our inability to make the right choices. And even when we do make the right choices, it may not be for the right reason (nor do we have the power to carry them out).

Complete deceit

The whole arena of addiction is filled with deceit. It is deceitful through and through. People deceive others to indulge. Satan deceives people into thinking that these addictions can provide us with what we need. We deceive *ourselves* concerning their use. People deceive and manipulate others so that they can continue to indulge in their addiction. People cover or hide their addictions from others.

Deceit is within the nature of addictions. The only way we can discern the truth is through Jesus Christ. Jesus said to those who believed in Him, "If you continue in my word, then you are my disciples indeed and you shall know the truth, and the truth will make you free" (John 8:32). It is only through an abiding relationship with Jesus Christ that we are free of deceit.

Chapter 4
D. The Real You
We are all vulnerable to addictions

Perhaps you have been so engulfed in an addiction that you can't believe the trouble that you've gotten yourself into. You are wondering where it all began. Some may say that it doesn't matter, "Just stop", they say. "You're gambling away your future. You are an insult to God and the people who love you…" Perhaps, it would be necessary for *some* people to grasp an understanding of the origin of addiction to begin their life of sobriety. If there is one thing that I can say beyond a shadow of a doubt is that **if we do not get a proper view of *ourselves*, we will not be able to maintain a life of abstinence.**

Let no man think more highly of himself than he ought to, but to think soberly.
(Rom. 12:3)

The fact is **we are not as wise as we sometimes think ourselves to be. We are not as powerful as we sometimes think. In fact, Proverbs 3:7 tells us not to be wise in our own eyes. If we do not see ourselves properly, we will not see God accurately either.** In his exposition of the names of Christ, Herbert Lockyer explains why it is that Jesus Christ is referred to as "The Way".

> "Man is lost in sin, and does not know the road back to God. Isaiah reminds us, that, "*All* we like sheep have gone astray," and in our desperation we have tried to carve out roads of our own. "There is a way which seemeth right unto a man, but the end thereof are the ways of death" (Proverbs 14:12; 16:25).

When in certain circumstances, we are apt to say, "Well, that is not my way of doing this," implying a different mode of operation. But in the matter of our salvation and eternal destiny there is no choice of ways – only one *way*, even Christ, through whom alone we can receive eternal life (1 John 5:11-13)."

In his 95 Theses for pure reformation Mike Cleveland says that "the one trapped in sexual idolatry does not see God properly, therefore he does not perceive spiritual truth accurately". Cleveland uses the phrase "hypnotic power" to describe the effect that the addiction has on some. "It is as if they have found some secret power, all without depending on God. But appearances deceive", says he. "Any time we are finding life, meaning or joy apart from our Creator, our growing alienation from Him will only lead to misery", says Ed Welch "Disillusionment often follows naïve admiration" is a phrase penned by John Piper.

A natural born fact

It may be shocking to some, but the fact is, **it is in our natures to seek after addictions/idols. John Calvin is quoted as saying that the heart of man is an idol factory.** Again, it is natural for people to be involved with addictions. There are several Bible passages that support this.

This know also, that in the last days perilous times shall come. For men shall be lovers of their own selves, covetous…lovers of pleasures more than lovers of God.
2 Timothy 3:1-4 (KJV)

But the natural man receiveth not the things of the Spirit of God: for they are foolishness unto Him: neither can he know them...
1 Corinthians 2:14 (KJV)

Now the works of the flesh are manifest, which are these: adultery, fornication, uncleanness, lasciviousness, idolatry, witchcraft...drunkenness...
Galatians 5:19-20 (KJV)

Anyone can become addicted to one thing or another. It is within the nature of man to sin. Given the right circumstances, any of us could become guilty of some of the most detestable acts of sins. The apostle Paul was a godly man, yet in Romans 7:18, he said, "For I know that in me [that is, in my flesh,] dwelleth no good thing; for to will is present with me; but how to perform that which is good I find not."

Sinful nature

By now, I know that you are probably tired of all the negativity. I want to get to the more 'favorable' message of the power and forgiveness that is offered to all that turn to Christ. Yet and still, for us to develop an appreciation for the things of God we must consider how lost we are without Him.

Just as I have said, it is in our nature to sin (we all have a sinful nature). The Bible teaches that it was by Adam that sin entered into the world (Romans 5:12). It is because we are in this realm of sin, under its reign and rule, that we begin to sin from infancy. We developed sinful habits and a sinful character.

Again, Dr. Wayne Mack states that, "Christ-centered counseling involves understanding the nature and courses of our human difficulties, understanding the ways we are unlike Christ in our values, aspirations, desires, thoughts, feelings, choices, attitudes, actions, and responses. Resolving those sin-related difficulties includes being redeemed and justified through Christ, receiving God's forgiveness through Christ, and acquiring from Christ the enabling power to replace unChristlike (sinful) patterns of life with Christlike, godly ones."

Giving in to the flesh

We become deeply involved with drug abuse, overeating, gambling addiction... because we give into our fleshly nature. This is why Jesus said that if anyone wanted to follow him, they must deny themselves daily (Luke 9:23). Jesus also told his disciples to "watch and pray, for the spirit indeed is willing but the flesh is weak" (Matthew 26:41). "Because sin and unbelief have warped the mind of man, he is in constant need of guidance and advice from above (1 Kings 3:7-10). What a relief to know that there is a Counsellor able to answer our questions, solve our riddles, and relieve us of our perplexity!", says Herbert Lockyer.

Defilement and deceit

Jesus said, "out of the heart of men proceed evil thoughts, adulteries, fornications... covetousness, wickedness... foolishness: all these evil things come from within, and defile the man" (Mark 7:21-23). As I have already mentioned, the Bible says that the heart is deceitful and no one understands it but God (Jeremiah 17:9-10). It is impossible to fight against something you can't understand.

Peter thought he knew his own heart. When Jesus said that everyone would be offended because of him, Peter said that though everyone else might be offended of Christ, he would never be offended (Matthew 26:31-35). Have you ever said that you would never indulge again? Never put anything beyond your selfish, sinful nature! **But for the grace of God**, anyone can become *involved with or return to drugs*, **alcohol, prostitution, sodomy, theft, murder, rape, etc. Anyone.** Peter, later, found out the weakness of his flesh, as he denied Christ three times (Matthew 26:69-75).

We can easily deceive ourselves into thinking that we love God as we should, until our faith is put to the test. John Piper has stated that, "**God wills to know the actual, lived-out reality of our preference for him over all things.** And he wills that we have the testimony of our own authenticity through acts of actual preference of God over his gifts." This is why I recommend fasting for those who are working on breaking the chains of addiction as well.

On your own

In Luke 21:34, Jesus said to "take heed to yourselves, lest at any time your hearts be weighted down with carousing, drunkenness, and the cares of this life." "**Addictions… don't just happen to us. We choose them. After a while, the addiction chooses us and we feel like slaves, but it is** *voluntary* **slavery.** Even with all the misery they bring, addictions do something for us." (Welch) We are often lured into sin as a frog in a pot of water boiling ever so slowly. If you place a frog in a pot of water that is room temperature and put the pot on the stove, *gradually* heating the water until it boils, the frog will boil to death before noticing the change of temperature. We are vulnerable to sin in this same fashion.

An underlying factor

Whether we resist temptation or yield to sin depends on our desires. Puritan Thomas Manton described our condition as such;

> **"Ever since the fall of man in the Garden of Eden man has listened to his desires more than his reasoning. When God created man, the reason, the emotion, and the will all worked in perfect harmony. Reason led way in the understanding of God's will, the will consented to God's will, and the emotions delighted in doing it. But with the entrance of sin into man's soul, these three faculties began to work at cross purposes to one another and to God."**

It's no wonder why Peter warned believers of Christ to "abstain from fleshly lusts which wage war against the soul" (1 Peter 2:11). 1 Thessalonians 5:19 says not to quench the Spirit of God. Without a doubt, the Spirit of God is given to all believers to protect us from *ourselves*.

Because Adam disobeyed God, sin entered into the world. "Thus, our reason [or understanding] was darkened (Ephesians 4:18), our desires were entangled (Ephesians 2:3), and our wills perverted (John 5:40). With the new birth our reason is again enlightened, our affections and desires redirected, and our wills subdued." Yet, it doesn't happen all of a sudden; it's something we grow into. (Bridges)

Beyond our own nature

It takes supernatural power to overcome temptation. This power comes from none other than Jesus Christ. Acts 4:12 says that there is no salvation outside of Christ: "For there is none other name under heaven given among men, whereby we must be saved." Through an ongoing relationship with Jesus Christ we are saved from being overtaken by temptations.

You don't have to be as the prodigal son, who was looking to feed on the husks that the swine ate (Luke 15:16). Jesus said that He came that you might have life and that you might have it more abundantly (John 10:10). Just as Moses pleaded with the Israelites, God is speaking these words to us:

> *I call heaven and earth to record this day against
> you, that I set before you life and death, blessing
> and cursing: therefore choose life, that both thou
> and thy seed may live; that thou mayest love the
> Lord thy God, and that thou mayest obey His voice,
> and that thou mayest cleave unto Him: for He is thy
> life.*
> **Deuteronomy 30:19-20 (KJV)**

Jesus Christ is still the way, the truth and the life (John 14:6).

Christ alone

The only way to stop drinking and drugging is through God's power and grace. ... Some don't even <u>recognize</u> that it was *by God's power and grace* that they were able to quit. Some are blessed with this power, even though they have not asked Christ to be their Savior. Just because you abstain from an addiction does not mean that you are pleasing to God. Romans 8:8 say that "they that are in the flesh cannot please God." God is not going to allow you into heaven because you have stopped drinking, drugging, viewing pornography. The only way to have peace with God is through Jesus Christ (Romans 5:1).

<u>Rejecting Christ is worst habit there is.</u> Hebrews 11:6 says that without faith it is impossible to please God. Jesus said that unless your righteousness exceeds the righteousness of the scribes and Pharisees, you will not enter the kingdom of heaven (Matthew 5:20). We cannot rely upon our own righteousness to save us. We need the righteousness of Christ to be saved from the wrath of God and to live a life that is pleasing to God.

For He (God) hath made Him who knew no sin (Christ) to be sin for us, that we might be the righteousness of God in Him.
2 Corinthians 5:21 (KJV)

What other proof do you need?

Are you convinced that you have no power over temptation, in and of yourself? Unless you are thoroughly convinced of this fact, you will look for answers apart from God and rely on your own strength to live a wholesome life. One of the safeguards against falling prey to the temptation of substance abuse and other sinful habits is to make a practice of confessing that we have no control over temptation. We should never allow the deceitfulness and enchantment of sin to fool us into thinking that *we* are in control. This is where repentance begins (our next phase).

Phase 2

Repent

A. Definition and Dynamics
B. Acts (Abstinence, fasting and communion)

Chapter 5
Definition and dynamics of repentance

By now you are probably tired of looking at the ugliness of addiction and are ready to see where change begins. And that's just what repentance is- change. **The biblical definition of repentance is to turn from self and follow Christ**. Repentance is a complete reversal of one's attitude and values. Some of the other definitions are as follows;

Baker Bible Dictionary

> To turn from evil, and to turn to the good. We are to abandon "both evil intentions and evil deeds, and both motive and conduct are to be radically changed." **To repent and to convert involves obedience to God's revealed will, placing trust in him, turning away from all evil and ungodliness**.

Eaton's Bible Dictionary

> To change one's mind and purpose, as the result of after knowledge.

Nave's Topical Bible

> A complete reversal of one's attitude and values, i.e. a turning toward God, attributed to God.

Dudley J. Delffs says that "to repent is to come to your senses. It is not so much something you do as something that happens." **True repentance spends less time looking at the**

48

past and saying, "I'm sorry," than to the future and saying "Wow!" – Frederick Buchner, *Wishful Thinking*

In a book titled "Manhood Restored: How the Gospel makes Men Whole", Eric Mason says that we have four options in our dealings with sin.

Option #1: You can deny that it is sin and accept it as normal behavior.
Option #2: You can attempt to excuse it or justify it.
Option #3: You can hate it and suffer under the guilt of it.
Option #4: You can repent and be cleansed from it.

In his book "The Doctrine of Repentance", Thomas Watson stated that the six ingredients of repentance are:

1. Sight of sin
2. Sorrow of sin
3. Confession of sin
4. Shame of sin
5. Hatred for sin
6. Turning from sin

Watson stated that "if any one is left out it loses its virtue."

Conviction and repentance

As it has been already stated, repentance begins with a change of mind, as the Spirit of God shows us, convinces us of the truth about sin and points us to Christ. As I said before, since God has created us with the ability to reason and the capacity to understand, then, we are able to form convictions over <u>addictions</u>. Contrary to what I once believed,

conviction is not the same as condemnation (although, *without* repentance convictions <u>lead</u> to condemnation). A conviction is *simply* something that we have discovered to be true. Convictions concern the issues of life, as presented by the holy scripture through the Holy Spirit of God, and how they are to be applied to our lives. Thus, we have the encouragement that is found in Ps 32:8-9 which says, I will instruct and teach you in the way that you shall go: I will guide you with my eye. Be not as the horse, or as the mule, which have no <u>understanding</u>: whose mouth must be held in with bit and bridle, lest they come near unto thee. The Lord God has made us in His own image. We are different from animals that only respond out of impose. It is not within God's will for us to be "party animals". animals that only respond out of impose. It is not within God's will for us to be "party animals".

Such a conviction requires a turning away from self, and dependence on God and His grace. Perhaps there's no simpler definition of repentance than the life process of turning away from self and toward our Father. This kind of faith requires believing that our Creator is authoring a masterpiece tapestry of all our realities beyond the mere landscape of what we can see and feel. When we're committed to knowing, loving, and trusting God beyond our circumstances, then we begin movement in a different direction. We realize our selfish agendas of feeling safe, comfortable, and happy all the time are not priorities from God's perspective. He's committed to a much deeper, much more radical love of our souls. Our transformation into Christlikeness (sanctification) takes precedence over our comfort and convenience.

A Repentant Heart- Dudley J. Delffs

The Process of Repentance

It is faith in God's word (His point of view) as well as the recognition of Who God is that leads us to repentance. Romans 2:4 states that the goodness of God leads to repentance. The change that is necessary has been given many different labels. Some of these terms are more accurate than others. Not only that, everyone has an option as to their degree of commitment towards change. There are many words that can be used to describe the process of turning from an addiction.

Recovery Sobriety Restoration Healing Set free
Maturity Growth Holiness Sanctified   .
Deliverance Reconciliation Being made whole
Revival Transformation Being saved
(Personally, I prefer the words repentance, transformation and sanctification.)

In terms of dealing with addictions, I believe that **2 Corinthians 7:11** has a lot to offer. The following is a section from "The Doctrine of Repentant" by way of explanation (pp. 93-95 lists seven adjuncts or effects of repentance laid down in 2 Corinthians 7:11).

For behold this selfsame thing, that ye sorrowed after a godly sort, what carefulness it wrought in you, yea, what clearing of yourselves, yea, what indignation, yea, what fear, yea, what vehement desire, yea, what zeal, yea, what revenge!

1. **Carefulness**
   The Greek word signifies a solicitous diligence or careful shunning all temptations to sin.

2. **Clearing of yourselves**
   The Greek word is 'apology'…the repenting soul will not let sin lie festering in his conscience but judges himself for his sin.

3. **Indignation**
   He that repents of sin, his spirit rises against it, as one's blood rises at the sight of him whom he mortally hates.

4. **Fear**
   A tender heart is ever a trembling heart. He is afraid to come near sin any more. He is afraid to lose God's favour which is better than life. He is afraid lest, after his heart has been soft, the waters of repentance should freeze and he should harden in sin again.

5. **Vehement desire**
   As sour sauce sharpens the appetite, so the bitter herbs of repentance sharpen desire. But what does the penitent desire? He desires more power against sin and to be released from it. In short, he desires to be with Christ, as everything desires to be in its center.

6. **Zeal**
   Desire and zeal are fitly put together to show that true desire puts forth itself in zealous endeavor. How does the penitent bestir himself in the business of salvation! How does he take the kingdom of heaven by force (Matt. 11:12)! Zeal quickens the pursuit after glory. Zeal makes a repenting soul persist in godly sorrow against all discouragements and oppositions whatsoever.

7. <u>Revenge</u>

A true penitent pursues his sins with a holy malice. A true child of God seeks to be revenged most of those sins which have dishonoured God most.

You will notice that every one of the effects of repentance listed in 2 Cor. 7:11 are attitudes backed by actions. God is very much concerned about our attitudes. We see this as far back as Genesis chapter four as God reasoned with Cain.

And the LORD said unto Cain, <u>Why art thou wroth? And why is thy countenance fallen?</u> If thou doest well, shalt thou not be accepted? and if thou doest not well, sin lieth at the door...
Genesis 4:6-7 (KJV)

An Attitude of Brokenness

While God leads us in establishing and maintaining an intimate relationship with Himself, our brokenness becomes one of the greatest attitudes. Brokenness requires humility. Brokenness gives us insight. Most importantly, God approves (even seeks) our brokenness. There is a direct correlation between idolatry and *hardheartedness*. Edward P. Meadors even has a book titled "Idolatry and the Hardening of the Heart". Since, the opposite of a hard heart is a broken heart then for us to thoroughly repent from idolatry we must have a broken heart.

> *The sacrifices of God are a broken spirit: a broken and a contrite heart, O God, Thou wilt not despise.*
> **Psalm 51:17 (KJV)**

For thus saith the high and lofty One that inhabiteth eternity, whose name is Holy; I dwell in the high and holy place, with him also that is of a contrite and humble spirit, to revive the spirit of the humble, and to revive the heart of the contrite ones. **Isaiah 57:15 (KJV)**

I have gained a lot of insight on brokenness through a book by Charles Stanley titled, "The Blessings of Brokenness". Some of the main points are listed below.

Chapter One is titled "Broken and Blessed?"
Running from or facing pain?
A perfect vessel

Chapter Two is titled "God Wants the Best for Us".
God always acts out of love.
Chastisement versus punishment

Chapter Three is titled "Why We are Broken".
Something has to die for life to begin.
God wants to set our goals.
We are Christ's workmanship.

Chapter Four is titled "The Obstacles to Brokenness".
Chapter Five is titled "What Does It Mean to be Made Whole?"

Chapter Six is titled "The Development of Spiritual Maturity"

Chapter Seven is titled "The Process of Breaking".
Chapter Eight is titled "Our Protest Against Brokenness".

Chapter Nine is titled "Preparation to Bear Much Fruit".

Chapter Ten is titled "The Promise of Blessing".

Brokenness, humility and pride

The true aim of brokenness is to make us humble enough to side with God. Pride is the one thing that prevents us from humbling ourselves. Edward P. Meadors wisely states;

> *"We usually do not think of pride as an idol. And yet the inclination to place one's self in the place of God is endemic to human nature. All human beings have the natural inclination to think a lot more about themselves than they think about God. It is therefore true that human beings in practice think and act as if they themselves are more important than God. Thus, if thinking and acting are valid indicators, human beings attribute more worth to themselves than to God."*

Meadors goes on to say that "repentance thus occurs out of an awareness that one's true value and worth is only discovered in a peaceful and honest relationship with one's Creator and not from servitude to one's own creation— whether material or mental".

A Summary of Repentance

Repentance is an act of self-denial. It is to surrender to the kingdom of God, to relinquish my own 'power', and to

55

stop seeking glory for myself. The need for repentance can be expressed in so many ways. Repentance determines our intimacy with the Almighty. This is because one of the components of repentance is confession. To confess to God means to say the same thing that God is saying about a matter. Repentance sets us apart from the world. Repentance is a by-product of reverence leading to purity. Repentance calls for priorities while restoring order and manageability.

The lack of repentance can be very dangerous. The alternative to repentance is to perish according to 2 Peter 3:9. It is through 2 Timothy 2: 24-26 that we learn gentle instruction leads to repentance, repentance is a thing that is granted by God, repentance leads to a knowledge of the truth, through repentance people come to their senses, and that it is through repentance that people escape the trap of the devil.

Revelation 3:18-19 teaches us that repentance is the result of counsel from the Wonderful Counselor (Jesus Christ). We, also, learn that repentance produces spiritual health and wealth and that rebuke and chastisement bring about repentance. In his wonderful book titled, "How to Help People Change", Jay Adams states, **"In all counseling change is a matter of greater or lesser love toward Him."**

Last, but not least, I don't think that you will find any place in the Bible that does not refer to repentance wherever revival is mentioned. I know that this is a lot to digest so I suggest that you read this 'summary' over carefully (again and again). Also, be sure to read Appendix E which includes a detailed outline on repentance from the scriptures.

Chapter 6
A. <u>Acts of Repentance</u>
(abstinence, fasting, and communion)

In our last chapter, we became familiar with the definition of repentance as well as some of the things that go along with repentance in a general manner. In this chapter, we will discuss some specific *actions* that addicts would be wise to perform during their repentance. Yet and still, these actions are not for addicts alone. The three acts that I propose are **abstinence, fasting, and communion.**

1. Abstinence

Perhaps, it goes without saying that to repent from an addiction one must <u>abstain</u> from the addiction, but we'll just throw it in for the sake of clarity, as well as giving us the opportunity to discuss things like prolonged sobriety, temptation, dual addiction, etc.

Making a clean break

We must make a clean break of idolatry <u>without any reservations</u>. We must be as decisive as Joshua in turning from idols.

If it is disagreeable in your sight to serve the Lord, choose for yourselves today whom you will serve: whether the gods which your fathers served which were beyond the river, or

*the gods of the Amorites in whose land you are living; but
as for me and my house, we will serve the Lord.*
Joshua 24:15, NAS

The choice is up to you. Israel faced the same decision in Elijah's day.

And Elijah came near to all the people and said, "How long will you hesitate between two opinions?" If the Lord is God, follow Him; but if Baal, follow him. (1 Kings 18:21).

Where we once gave our lives to idolatry, we are called to give our lives to God. We must not be half-hearted in our resignation of idolatry either. We combine our **commitment against idolatry with a sound commitment to follow Christ**. John 6:66-69 is an example of how determined we should be about following Jesus Christ.

*After this, many of his disciples drew back [returned to
their old associations] and no longer accompanied him.
Jesus said to the twelve, will you also go away? [And do
you desire to leave me?] Simon Peter answered, Lord, to
whom shall we go? You have the words [the message] of
eternal life. And we have come to know [surely] that you
are the holy one of God, the Christ [the anointed one], the
son of the living God.*
John 6:66-69, Amplified Version

*Then Jacob said unto his household, and to
all that were with him, put away the strange
gods that are among you, and be clean, and
change your garments.*
Genesis 35:2

*Now therefore fear the Lord, and serve Him in
sincerity and in truth; and put away the gods which
your fathers served on the other side of the flood,
and in Egypt; and serve the Lord.*
Joshua 24:14

The words "put away" carry a certain meaning. Put away—to turn off, decline, depart, eschew, go (aside), be past, pluck away, remove, turn (aside, away), withdraw. The idea of changing garments in Genesis 35:2 is significant to the idea brought forth in the New Testament of putting off the "old man" and putting on the new man found in Christ (Ephesians 4:21-24; Colossians 3:9-10). Some of the Greek words used in these passages had to do with changing clothes. Back in Biblical days, the average person would rarely obtain a new set of clothing. By the time they did get a change of clothing, their old clothes were usually pretty raggedy and soiled. As it was a joy and a delight for these people to put off their old clothes and put on the new, so it should be for us to turn from every addiction and cleave to the Lord.

In his book titled, "Hard to Believe", John MacArthur states that "Becoming a Christian means being sick of your sin, longing for forgiveness and rescue from present evil and future hell, and affirming your commitment to the lordship of Christ to the point where you are willing to forsake everything".

Tony Evans uses an illustration in his book *Returning to Your First Love* of the irony in being indecisive about following Jesus. It is said that the Christian's relationship with Christ is like that of a husband and wife. Evans says,

"Imagine a couple who come to me for counseling and the husband says, "Look, I'm not sure whether I want my wife or this other woman. I love them both.

But until I decide, I want my wife to stick with me. I want her to keep cooking and cleaning for me. I want her to be understanding. I want her to serve me and be faithful to me while I decide whether I want her or the other woman. My wife has some good qualities and meets my needs. But, so does this other woman. So, I want my wife to keep being the wonderful wife she is while I decide whether I want her or the other one." This will not work in marriage, nor does it work out in our relationship with the Lord Jesus. Matthew 6:24 explains what happens when a person's allegiance for the Lord is divided. No one can serve two masters; for either he will hate the one and love the other, or he will stand by and be devoted to the one and despise and be against the other. You cannot serve God and mammon [deceitful riches, money, possessions, or whatever is trusted in]. **Matthew 6:24, Amplified Version**

The believers mentioned in Acts 19:18-19 were a tremendous example of those who discarded any reservation towards ungodliness.

And many that believed came, and confessed, and showed their deeds. Many of them also which used curious arts brought their books together, and burned them before all men: and they counted the price of them, and found it fifty thousand pieces of silver.
Acts 19:18-19

Theirs was an expression of how the Lord is worthy of all we have, and all that we are!

Complete abstinence

By complete abstinence I mean that you **do not partake of the addiction, get rid of everything that is associated with the addiction and to abstain from even reminiscing over the addiction.** It has been wisely said by Narcotics Anonymous that "one is too many and a thousand is too much" when it comes to indulging in an addiction.

One of things that I used to ask myself before returning to an addiction (after abstaining for a while) was how long would I continue with the addiction. Well, the answer to that is always, "I don't know". Nobody knows how long they will indulge in an addiction so long as they continue to practice that addiction.

Practice is a key word (but we'll get back to that later). It has, also, been said that "sin will keep you longer than you intended to stay and cost you more than you can pay". I won't even talk about how addictions *progress* as long as we indulge (in fact, we discussed that in my section on the uselessness of idols). I realize that we all experience moments of temptation, and that is something that I will discuss next. I often tell people that **it is actually easier for one to abstain from their addiction then to return to it** (particularly when they have not indulged for some time).

Temptation

Just as I said earlier, it takes supernatural power to overcome temptation. This power comes from none other than Jesus Christ. Acts 4:12 says that there is no salvation in any other: "For there is none other name under heaven given among men, whereby we must be saved." Through an ongoing relationship with Jesus Christ we are saved from being overtaken by temptations. Through the Lord Jesus Christ (the power and wisdom of God), we can live a life that is pleasing to God. The wisdom of God causes us to think right. Colossians 2:3 tells us that in Christ are hidden all the treasures of wisdom and knowledge. Where there is no counsel, the people fall (Proverbs 11:14). The best advice we can get is directly from Christ. He does, however, use others to help make wise decisions also. The words of the wise are as goads, and as nails fastened by the master of assemblies, which are given by one shepherd (Ecclesiastes 12:11). Proverbs 11:14 also says that in the multitude of counselors there is safety. By personally knowing Christ, we are able to directly consult Him at any time, in any place, in order to gain a sober mind. The really great thing is that Jesus fully understands.

For we have not a high priest, which cannot be touched with the feeling of our infirmities; but was in all points tempted like as we are, yet without sin. Let us therefore come boldly unto the throne of grace, that we may obtain mercy, and find grace to help in time of need. **Hebrews 4:15-16**

Jesus shows us how to put things into perspective. God is not the author of confusion (like idols are). No Jesus, no peace; know Jesus, know peace. Sometimes temptations can be overwhelming. Psalm 61:2 reveals how David knew the value of consulting Christ.

From the end of the earth will I cry unto thee, when my heart is <u>overwhelmed</u>: lead me to the rock [Christ] that is higher than I.
Psalm 61:2

Ultimately the means of dealing with temptation involves the principle that is laid down in 2 Corinthians 10:4-5 (KJV).

For the weapons of our warfare are not carnal, but mighty through God to the pulling down of strongholds; Casting down imaginations and every high thing that exalts itself against the knowledge of God, and bringing every thought into captivity to the obedience of Christ.

Dual Addiction

Often times, there are other addictions that accompany the *primary* addiction that people participate in. For instance, drug addiction is often accompanied by some sort of sexual addiction, cigarette smoking goings with drinking, and so on.

While some may say that people need to take care of one issue at a time, I am stating that the believer in Christ must forsake anything that they are convinced within themselves would be an offence to God. I'm not saying that this is easy, but it's biblical. Anything that comes between us and God must go.

Now, with some addictions there are certain physical symptoms that go with withdrawal that can be life-threatening. In these instances, it would be necessary for individuals to seek help from the medical community so that they can safely begin the process of abstinence.

As I said, I know that it won't be easy for people to give up all their addictions at once, but the scriptures tell us that with God all things are possible. **As quiet as it's kept, if we do not deal with each and every thing that we know to be** offensive to God then we do not hear His voice as well. As a result of not hearing His voice so well we become vulnerable to drifting from the safety that He affords. If we continue to engage in certain behavior (outside of our *primary* addiction), it may eventually lead us back.

Not only does the addict have to give up every addiction that is displeasing to God, they may have to give up some things that are not addictive within themselves yet associated with their addiction(s). There may be things that remind them of their addiction, there may be people that they must not associate with (at least not so closely, in some cases not at all). Just think of how Abram was called by God to leave his homeland because of their idolatry. God wanted him all to Himself. The same is true for you. And isn't He worthy?

Radical Repentance

Repentance is all about radical change. The radical change that God wants for us is to occur on various levels (mentally, spiritually, physically, socially...). In terms of abstinence we are dealing with the physical aspect of repentance (for the most part). Later we will discuss the spiritual aspect of repentance as we deal with communion (with God and others). The next aspect of repentance binds the physical with the spiritual like nothing else. This aspect of repentance is what is known as fasting.

2. Fasting

Repentance and fasting seem to go hand in hand in the scriptures. Many times, where repentance is mentioned in scripture there is also fasting. Take Jonah 3:3-8 (KJV) for instance.

So Jonah arose, and went unto Nineveh, according to the word of the Lord. Now Nineveh was an exceeding great city of three days' journey. And Jonah began to enter into the city a day's journey, and he cried, and said, Yet forty days, and Nineveh shall be overthrown. So the people of Nineveh believed God, and proclaimed a fast, and put on sackcloth, from the greatest of them even to the least of them. For word came unto the king of Nineveh, and he arose from his throne, and he laid his robe from him, and covered him with sackcloth, and sat in ashes. And he caused it to be proclaimed and published through Nineveh by the decree of the king and his nobles, saying, Let neither man nor beast, herd nor flock, taste any thing: let them not feed, nor drink water: But let man and beast be covered with sackcloth, and cry mightily unto God: yea, let them turn every one from his evil way, and from the violence that is in their hands.

Practice

Am I saying that people *have to* fast in order to develop a life of sobriety? It sure wouldn't hurt. Since fasting is a practice of denying ourselves, then it can be of great benefit to those who were previously engage in the self-absorbing life of addiction. (Though I just called fasting a practice, we could just as well call it a habit). **It is very important for those who are turning from addictions to replace bad habits with good habits.**

Once again, fasting is an act of self-denial. Such a practice must be done <u>unto God</u> as an expression of His worthiness. I recommend a book called "A Hunger for God' by John Piper to all readers who are serious about implementing the practice of fasting into their lives. One of the statements that Piper makes is that "Christian fasting is a test to see what desires control us". One of the other thoughts that Piper conveys is that <u>our fast unto God is telling God that we want Him more than anything</u> (even food and water). I would have to say that whether it comes to fasting or turning from sin, we either deny ourselves or we deny Christ (it's just that simple).

Specifics

By fasting I am referring to abstaining from food and/or water for a certain period of time. Fasting can be done as a group or by a single individual. Your fasting may be something that you decide on your own, led by another believer (usually a leader), or solely led by the Spirit of God (sometimes we are not aware that it was His leading anyway).

There are all kinds of variations to fasting as well. It can be said that fasting is the abstinence from anything that is legitimate in and of itself, for some spiritual purpose. You may choose the amount of time you intend on fasting in advance or decide as you go. You can decide whether you will engage in a partial fast or a 'strict' fast. A partial fast is one in which you decide upon abstaining from <u>various</u> foods (usually the participant abstains from meats for a period of time). A strict fast is the practice of abstaining from <u>all</u> foods (and drinking only water). I would advise those who have health conditions to consult their physician before fasting.

The main thing is that **a fast is meant to be God centered rather than self-centered.**

Advantages

No matter what kind of fast you engage upon, <u>a fast is something that is different than the ordinary</u>. That's just type of life that God is calling us to have (different). You might say that a fast can be a statement or an agreement with God that we are going to do things differently and that we are giving ourselves completely over to Him. Fasting, also, gives us the opportunity to shut out the distractions of things that are earthly. Many of which are not evil (in and of themselves), yet they have the ability to lure our attention beyond our advantage. Jesus said, "Be careful, or your hearts will be weighed down with dissipation, drunkenness and the anxieties of life, and that day will close on you unexpectedly like a trap." (Luke 20:34). Fasting gives us the ability of being more alert (watchful).

Another advantage to **fasting is that it teaches us to suffer**. Suffering is important to our spiritual growth. Suffering gives us the opportunity to become more like Christ. Christ *himself* grew through suffering.

Though he were a Son, yet learned he obedience by the things which he suffered
Hebrews 5:8

<u>**Suffering teaches us things that we would not learn in any other manner**</u>. For the person repenting from an addiction suffering must become more of a reality. Whenever someone indulges in an addiction (of any kind) he

or she is attempting to avoid suffering (in one form or another).

Fasting helps the believer to abide in Christ (to stay in fellowship with the Lord). This is not only the key to sobriety, it is *actually* the main goal (as stated before in so many words). 1 John 2:28 says, "And now, little children, abide in him; that, when he shall appear, we may have confidence, and not be ashamed before him at his coming." Abiding in Christ is maintained through our next act of repentance, which is communion.

In addition, there is rest for the body in fasting because some of our organs do not have to function as they normally do. There is rest for our souls in fasting. We do not have to concern ourselves with the acquiring, preparation and disposal of foods. Fasting allows us the opportunity to slow down. In fact, it is highly recommended that you move slower during a fast as you may experience a decrease in energy. Fasting allows our bodies to detoxify as well. This could be proving to be an important element for those who have abused substances.

3. Communion

By communion I am not referring to partaking of the Lord's Supper (although it can be included the discussion). By communion I am referring to the fellowship between us and God, and our fellowship with others (particularly those who have also put their faith in Christ). We will be looking at our relationship with God and our relationship with others separately. You may ask, "why didn't you just use the word 'fellowship'"? Well, I like the way that 'communion' indicates a *union* (a 'oneness').

Our fellowship with God can be simplified into three basic areas. **Listening to God, talking to God, and doing what God says.** This is all that is involved in our communion with God. Although volumes have been written on each, I can only provide a brief description of each. (I encourage each of my readers to seek out more extensive studies on these subjects, they are *some* of the core elements that are necessary for spiritual growth).

a. Fellowship with God

(1) Listening to God

All that God has to say to us is found in His Word. Sometimes He will speak directly to us, sometimes through someone else, and then, at other times He will speak through circumstances. But, however He speaks, it is always backed by His Word. Another clue to listening to God is that everything that God says is in some way or another connected to Jesus Christ. There are at least three reasons why everything that God says is connected to Jesus.

(a) Jesus is called the Word of God
In the beginning was the Word, and the Word was with God, and the Word was God.
John 1:1

(b) Jesus is God's final word to man
In the past God spoke to our forefathers through the prophets at many times and in various ways, but in these last days he has spoken to us by his Son...
Hebrews 1:1-2a

(c) All that we need (every answer) is found in Christ

His divine power has given us everything we need for life and godliness through our knowledge of him who called us by his own glory and goodness. Through these he has given us his very great and precious promises, so that through them you may participate in the divine nature and escape the corruption in the world caused by evil desires.
2 Peter 1:3-4

Listening to God forms a bond between us and God. Listening to God shows us the proper way of viewing and responding to things. Listening to God draws us away for worldly ideas (which lead to sin and ungodliness).

Do not conform any longer to the pattern of this world, but be transformed by the renewing of your mind.
Romans 12:2a

(2) Talking with God

Next is the communion of talking to God (better known as prayer). Prayers usually fall under four basic categories.

Adoration: Praising God.
Contrition: Asking for God's forgiveness.
Petition: Asking God for a favor.
Thanksgiving: Showing God gratitude.

One of the amazing things about prayer is that you are before the Lord as you pray. I did a study on all the times that this phrase (before the Lord) is mentioned and have found it to be quite interesting.

To be before the Lord (as I mentioned before) is the most sobering thing in all the universe. At the same time, being before the Lord can be either comforting or disturbing.

One of the most challenging things about prayer is that **as we talk to God we also listen to Him** so that we will be able to pray close to the way that He wants, hence we will be able to get a feel for what He has to say about our requests. Someone once said that prayer is letting God know that you're in on what He is doing. Here is where the element of meditation enters.

Meditation is closely associated with prayer, yet and still they are not always done at the same time. Merriam-Webster's definition of meditation is to engage in contemplation or reflection. Other words that describe meditation are to consider or ponder. Once again, I would encourage each reader to seek farther reading. I am not able to adequately cover some of the subjects that are presented.

(3) Doing what God says

When we do what God says we are communing with God in an intimate manner as well. When we do what God says with the right attitude, we are in agreement with Him. I like the way that this is expressed in the KJV with the use of the word "conversation" in various passages which is presented as "life, live, etc." in other versions. What we see is yet another method of communication between us and God. As we do what God says with the right kind of attitude, it is a practice of worship (as we are telling God that He is worthy of our obedience). This is what others 'hear' as well. And when we don't do as He says, or do it with a bad attitude, we are telling Him, as well as others, that He is not worthy. Here are some passages that express the idea I have just presented:

Negative (ungodly)

Among whom also we all had our **conversation** in times past in the lusts of our flesh, fulfilling the desires of the flesh and of the mind; and were by nature the children of wrath, even as others.
Ephesians 2:3

That ye put off concerning the former **conversation** the old man, which is corrupt according to the deceitful lusts.
Ephesians 4:22

Forasmuch as ye know that ye were not redeemed with corruptible things, as silver and gold, from your vain **conversation** received by tradition from your fathers.
1 Peter 1:18

And delivered just Lot, vexed with the filthy **conversation** of the wicked.
2 Peter 2:7

Positive

Only let your **conversation** be as it becometh the gospel of Christ.
Philippians 1:27a

For our **conversation** is in heaven; from whence also we look for the Saviour, the Lord Jesus Christ.

Philippians 3:20

Let your **conversation** be without covetousness.
Hebrews 13:5

Who is a wise man and endued with knowledge among
you? let him shew out of a good conversation his works
with meekness of wisdom.
James 3:13

But as he which hath called you is holy, so be ye holy in all
manner of **conversation**.
1 Peter 1:15

Having a good conscience; that, whereas they speak evil of
you, as of evildoers, they may be ashamed that falsely
accuse your good **conversation** in Christ.
1 Peter 3:16

Seeing then that all these things shall be dissolved, what
manner of persons ought ye to be in all holy **conversation**
and godliness.
2 Peter 3:11

b. Fellowship with others

Our repentance and rejoicing will never be complete
outside of our involvement with others in the body of Christ.
The rejoicing that we are able to share with others who are
leaning and depending on Jesus is of great power. It is here
that we have the promise of God's presence.

For where two or three come together in my name, there
am I with them.
Matthew 18:20

But thou art holy, O thou that inhabitest the praises of
Israel.
Ps. *22:3 (The Lord inhabits the praise of His people)*

Another advantage to our fellowship with other believers is the opportunity for each to be built up and encouraged in their faith. In fact, if you dive into the word of God enough, you will find that it is something that we cannot do without (see Eph. 4:11-13, 16 and 1 Cor. 12:14-26 for starters). I, actually, believe that **our intimacy with God largely depends on our intimacy with others**.

When it comes to fellowshipping with others the first thing that you must consider is the level on which you interact with various people. Just as you probably would not go home and try to talk to the dog about the complexities of your job, it would not be a good idea to stir up a conversation concerning spiritual matters with someone who does not know Christ. Jesus said in John 6:63 "It is the spirit that quickeneth; the flesh profiteth nothing: the words that I speak unto you, they are spirit, and they are life. And so, the fellowship that is necessary for repentance and growth is found in those who are in the body of Christ.

And so, you decide on the degree of intimacy that you will have with someone else. To say that you fellowship with someone while sitting next to them in church is quite different then inviting them into your home, meeting with them one on one, calling them up and talking about personal matters… While each level of fellowship has its place, to meet with someone on a more intimate level allows us to grow like none other. One is the opportunities that those who struggle with addictions has for a deeper level of intimacy is through a 'support group'. Appendix F gives you a closer look at what Christ-centered support groups are all about.

Practicing Repentance

And so, these acts of repentance are practices that lead to growth and maturity. They are the means of discarding all that would stand in the way of our relationship to God as well as others and prevent us from being a reflection of Jesus Christ. First there is the abstinence (naturally), and then the other two elements (supernatural) are fasting and communion. I call them practices because they become 'habits' (healthy habits). I refer to them as practices, also, because we never become prefect at it on this side of glory. The next phase that we are led to is rejoicing.

Phase III

<u>Rejoice</u>

Chapter 7
Rejoicing in the Lord

So far, we have looked at the necessity of reason when dealing with an addiction (first phase). Next, we discussed the elements and importance of repentance (second phase). In this third and final phase, we move on to rejoicing.

If we never experience the joy of the Lord in our repentance, then I doubt if we have really repented.

Biblical repentance is designed towards leading us to rejoice. An example is found in Acts 3:19.

Repent ye therefore, and be converted, that your sins may be blotted out, when the times of refreshing shall come from the presence of the Lord.

Remember, **repentance is not only means that we turn from sin, but that we turn _to_ Jesus!** In Jesus Christ there is joy. In his book titled "Counterfeit Gods", Timothy Keller says that

"**Rejoicing and repentance must go together. Repentance without rejoicing will lead to despair. Rejoicing without repentance is shallow and will only provide passing inspiration instead of deep change. Indeed, it is when we rejoice over Jesus's sacrificial love for us most fully that, paradoxically, we are most truly convicted of our sin. When we repent out of fear of consequences, we are not really sorry for the sin, but for ourselves... In fear-based repentance, we don't** learn to hate the sin for itself, and it doesn't lose its attractive power. We learn only to refrain from it for our own sake... Fear-based repentance makes us hate ourselves. Joy-based repentance makes us hate the sin."

The joy of the Lord

Many years ago, while attending an Alcoholics Anonymous meeting, I listened to a speaker who had such broken English that I thought that I heard him say that he was 'merciful' during the many times that he had stopped drinking and so he would go back to drinking time and time again. Over and over, the speaker said that he was "very merciful" when he stopped drinking. Towards the end of his speech, I finally realized that the speaker had been telling us that he had been "miserable" during those times of abstinence (without true fellowship with God). While God wants us to be merciful in our walk with Him, He does not want us to be miserable. George Muller said that, "the first great and primary business to which I ought to attend every day is have my soul happy in the Lord". Muller is credited for saying that, "our first duty as Christians is to get ourselves happy in God". Nehemiah 8:10 says that **the joy of the Lord is your strength**.

What good is repentance if it does not lead to joy? Deliverance is not complete without joy. Joy is what makes this formula of sanctification complete. **More than anything else, *Turning to God from Idols* is all about intimate fellowship with the Father through Jesus Christ while recognizing the glory of God**. One of Jesus closest disciples (John) said, "That which we have seen and heard declare we unto you, that ye also may have fellowship with us: and truly our fellowship is with the Father, and with His Son Jesus Christ. And these things write we unto you, **that your joy may be full**." (1 John 1:3-4, KJV).

The practice of joy

Now in case you are having problems finding joy, I do not want you to be in despair. **Joy is not something that you have to produce or manufacture**. Joy is the fruit of the Spirit (Gal. 5:22). By the same token, joy *is* a practice. A practice can also be defined as a habit. Whether good or bad, a habit becomes a lifestyle. And so, even if you have trouble with exhibiting joy, by making it a practice, through the aid of the Holy Spirit, you become better and better. One of the best ways of expressing the joy of the Lord is through music (which is discussed in Appendix F under starting a support group). Although it *is* a supernatural element, it starts to *seem* 'natural' over time. A long time ago, I heard that you can tell when you are growing as a Christian when to do what is right seems almost natural.

I was blessed to witness my dad to make joy a practice (although he was unable to walk for the last twenty years of his life). If there was one outstanding trait that everyone noticed about my dad was the smile that he had on his face each and every day that was produced by the joy that was in his heart. **He simply would not let anything come between his fellowship with the Father**. 1 Peter 1:8 explains how the believer's joy is based on the love that we have for Christ.

*Whom having not seen, ye love; in whom, though now ye
see him not, yet believing, ye rejoice with joy unspeakable
and full of glory.* (KJV)

Reverence and rejoicing

Yes, we are going to visit our old friend reverence again.
In fact, he really never left. In my attempt to simplify a
formula for dealing with addictions, I have found at least
four 'R's' that must be implemented. Those 'R's'are;
Reason, reverence, repentance, and rejoicing. If you would
go back to our definition for reverence, you will see that
reverence contains the element of rejoicing.

*Some of the ideas conveyed in the Strong Exhaustive
Concordance and Dictionary for reverence are;* **to prize
(fix valuation upon), splendor,** *esteem (esp. of the highest
degree), gaze, behold, take heed, bashfulness or modesty
(towards God), honor, and* **enjoy.**

What does it mean to rejoice?

I thought that you'd never ask. Rejoicing comes from joy.
Both Webster's Dictionary and Funk and Wagnalls Standard
Dictionary define 'rejoice' as being filled with joy. Joy is
defined in The Merriam Webster Dictionary as a feeling of
happiness that comes with success, good fortune, or a sense
of well-being. Also, defined as bliss, delight, enjoyment and
pleasure. Webster's Dictionary defines joy as a strong
feeling of great happiness, delight, a state or source of
contentment or satisfaction.

Funk and Wagnalls' defines joy as anything that causes delight or gladness.

Dictionary.com defines joy as the emotion of great delight or happiness caused by something exceptionally good or satisfying; keen pleasure; elation.

All in Christ

For the sake of brevity, I will not go into great detail as to how there is great joy that is found in Christ. I will only mention how that Jesus Christ provides the only means of forgiveness with God. That should produce joy. **Through the blood of Christ, providing forgiveness, we are given the greatness level intimacy with a God who is infinitely beyond all there is (including the idols we would embrace).** This is priceless. We have the promises of God through Christ. We have peace and contentment by walking with Christ. If the truth were known; **the joy that God gives in Christ is measureless.**

The fruit of the Spirit/supernatural

Make no mistake! Although the joy that I have been describing is a practice, it is not self-manufactured. The joy of the Lord is the fruit of the Spirit (therefore supernatural). For one thing, the joy of the Lord is not based on circumstances. Herbert Lockyer said, "An evident sign that we are living in harmony with the mind and will of the Holy Spirit is the way in which He can make us joyful – even when it seems there is nothing to sing about – "joyful in *all* our tribulation" (2 Corinthians 7:4).

Elements of Joy (with an emphasis on praise)

This leads us to the elements of joy. One of those elements being **contentment**. Contentment allows those who have 'chased' after idols to rest. Joy produces satisfaction with what God has given us. Very closely related to contentment is the element of **gratitude** or thanksgiving. We are not just satisfied with the things that God has provided us with, we are thankful.

Yet and still the two of these elements (contentment and gratitude) cannot exist without praise unto God. **Joy is full of praise**. Praise is essential to joy. This leads us right back to our theme of reverence as well. True reverence is always, always, always accompanied with praise. There is no such thing as reverence without praise, and there is no such thing as praise without reverence. And not only that, but our praise 'itself' is reverential. We are careful to praise God as He deserves (in a reverential manner, of the highest quality). But then, it is really a matter of how great the Lord is to us. It is no wonder that Peter exhorts believers to gird up the loins of our minds and Paul says to be renew by the transforming of our minds.

We need to see God in His greatness to reverence Him, and increase our reverence. In his series on fearing God, Dr. Tony Evans says that a great God deserves great respect and a little God receives little respect, honor. Evans says that if God is not all that great to us, then He will not get much reverence from us.

Delight

Another word that can be used for "joy" is delight. In the appendixes, you will find some references on "joy and rejoicing". I would like to close this chapter with some select verses on "delight". (Taken from the KJV).

Negative (ungodly)

They only consult to cast him down from his excellency: they **delight** in lies: they bless with their mouth, but they curse inwardly. Selah.
Psalm 62:4

How long, ye simple ones, will ye love simplicity? and the scorners **delight** in their scorning, and fools hate knowledge?
Proverbs 1:22

Who rejoice to do evil, and **delight** in the frowardness of the wicked;
Proverbs 2:14

Folly **delights** a man who lacks judgment, but a man of understanding keeps a straight course. Proverbs 15:21 (NIV)

A fool hath no **delight** in understanding, but that his heart may discover itself.
Proverbs 18:4

To whom shall I speak, and give warning, that they may hear? behold, their ear is uncircumcised, and

they cannot hearken : behold, the word of the
LORD is unto them a reproach; they have no
delight in it.
Jeremiah 6:10

Positive

For then shalt thou have thy **delight** in the
Almighty, and shalt lift up thy face unto God.
Job 22:26

Will he **delight** himself in the Almighty? will he
always call upon God?
Job 27:10

But his **delight** is in the law of the LORD; and in his
law doth he meditate day and night.   Psalm 1:2

Delight thyself also in the LORD; and he shall give
thee the desires of thine heart.   Psalm 37:4

I **delight** to do thy will, O my God: yea, thy law is
within my heart.
Psalm 40:8

I will **delight** myself in thy statutes: I will not forget
thy word.
Psalm 119:16

Thy testimonies also are my **delight** and my
counsellors.
Psalm 119:24

Yet they seek me daily, and **delight** to know my ways, as a nation that did righteousness, and forsook not the ordinance of their God: they ask of me the ordinances of justice; they take **delight** in approaching to God.
Isaiah 58:2

Then shalt thou **delight** thyself in the LORD; and I will cause thee to ride upon the high places of the earth, and feed thee with the heritage of Jacob thy father: for the mouth of the LORD hath spoken it.
Isaiah 58:14

Conclusion

Here we have a simple formula of dealing with addictions biblically. As the saying goes- "easier said than done". We have a difficult task before us. Though you may be struggling with one particular addiction, you can rest assured that there may be others that you have not noticed or one that may gain your future affections. Some addictions are accepted by society and yet hideous to God. Other addictions are neither socially acceptable nor pleasing to God. Those are the ones that people and usually most concerned about because they yield pain.

I urge you to be diligent in your studies and to be transparent before God, as well as others. I think that it is safe to say that you will find the elements of reason, repentance, and rejoicing within any and every 'program' that deals with addictions, in one form or another (although it may be expressed in other words). If these elements are not found in any one program, well, they should be. These same 'phases' often occur in the lives of those who never even engage in some type of 'formal' program. Reason leads to repentance and repentance leads to rejoicing. Let us once again take a look at each phase!

Reason

The reasoning that is needed in phase one is God's reasoning. As the scripture says, "There is a way that appears to be right, but in the end it leads to death." (Proverbs 14:12). Without God's reasoning, we never fully see the depth and the severity of addictions. If we do not see the depth and the severity of our addictions, I doubt if we

86

would want to make any changes. We must be in tune with the goals that God has for us. We must decide that we want to change in the way that God wants us to change, for the same reasons that God wants us to change. As we 'stand' before the Lord, we must consider our motives. That which honors God and benefits us best is done out of reverence towards God. It is within this reasoning that we discover how addictions not only dishonor God, they have no lasting value, and that all mankind is vulnerable to addictions. And the reason that addictions dishonor God is because they are idols.

In order to begin the process of change we need to be soundly convinced of the nature of our addictions. In this process we not only look at what we consider to be the 'assets' of our addictions, but their liabilities as well as their spiritual implications. It is with accurate judgment that we label addictions as idols because of the worship that is express towards them. Whenever we worship something or someone we make sacrifices, we relinquish control, we esteem praise, and we bestow trust.

Our reasoning leads us to the remarkable discovery that the scriptures have a lot to say about addictions. Personally, I believe that **if the word of God had nothing to say about addictions then God would not have created us**. We can, clearly see the various aspects of addictions displayed in the Bible in the form of idolatry most.

Repent

And so, if addiction is idolatry, then is it a sin. If addiction is a sin, then it is something that we can repent of. Repentance is to turn from self and to follow Christ. As the Spirit of God gives us conviction over addictions and concerning the truth of Jesus Christ, then we are led in repentance by the Word of God. Isaiah 55:7-9 says,

> **Let the wicked forsake his way, and the unrighteous man his thoughts: and let him return unto the Lord, and he will have mercy upon him; and to our God, for he will abundantly pardon. For my thoughts are not your thoughts, neither are your ways my ways, saith the Lord. For as the heavens are higher than the earth, so are my ways higher than your ways, and my thoughts than your thoughts.**
>
> ### (KJV)

This repentance is marked and led by brokenness as well. Keep in mind that our reverence for God is behind it all! Some of the most distinguishing characteristics of true repentance are listed in 2 Corinthians 7:11 as well. The brokenness that is necessary for repentance requires that we abandon our pride and practice humbling ourselves. The self-denial of repentance allows us the greatest intimacy with the Almighty that is humanly possible.

Repentance from an addiction towards Christ requires action. Abstinence and communion with God and with others are mandatory. Fasting is very highly recommended. Abstinence is to be done without any reservations We avoid anything that is even remotely associated with the addictions that we once clung to as Jude says, "hating even the garments spotted by flesh" (Jude 23). Upon our repentance, we will be tempted to return to our idols. Our fasting and communion with God and with others will give us the strength that we need to remain 'sober'.

Since fasting is an act of self-denial, then we can see why fasting was often done during biblical days in association with repentance. I cannot overemphasize the benefit of fasting for those of us that have once given ourselves to an addiction. Whatever form of fasting that we choose, so long as we do it out of reverence for God rather than for selfish reasons, then the Lord truly will take notice!

Could it be that the aim of repentance is really our fellowship with God as well as others (communion)? Did not Jesus say that the greatest commandment is to love the Lord your God with all your heart, your soul, and your mind and the second greatest is to love your neighbor as yourself? (Matthew 22:37-39). Also, the Westminster Shorter Catechism says that, "**Man's chief end is to glorify God, and to enjoy him forever**".

Our fellowship with God requires that we listen to God, we talk with God, and we do what God says. We make a choice of the people we fellowship with. We decide the degree of intimacy we have with others as well. An intimate involvement with a Bible-based support group is highly recommended for those who have been bound to addictions. Intimate involvement among all believers should be a common practice.

It is within our repentance that we put down bad habits and develop and practice good habits. The acts of repentance that I have given to you are the 'core' essentials when pulling down the strongholds of addictions. The lists of additions (good) habits are practically endless (exercise, volunteering, hobbies and so on).

Rejoice

And so, after we are led by God in our reasoning and repenting, He causes us to rejoice. We rejoice that we have an unbreakable bond with God because of the forgiveness of our sins through the blood of Christ. We rejoice that we are no longer slaves to sin through Christ (that includes idolatry or whatever else displeases God). We rejoice in the person that God has created us to be. We rejoice in the people that God has placed in our lives. We rejoice in the Lord. The joy that we have occurs automatically as a result of our repentance. As we walk in the Spirit, God blesses us with the fruit of the Spirit (which contains joy, Gal. 5:22). Although true joy can only be produced by the Spirit of God, it is also a practice that we are called to uphold. It is as any other blessing that God would have us to partake of that no one is able to keep us from having except us.

Have you found joy in an addiction? Probably not! Certainly not the joy that is found in Jesus! Here is reason to repent. God has so much in store for us! Eye hath not seen, nor ear heard, neither have entered into the heart of man, the things which God hath prepared for them that love him (1 Corinthians 2:9, KJV). God has expressed His love for us in so many ways, but the greatest demonstration of His love was when He gave us His Son. And so, let us show our love for God by rejecting the idols of addiction and clinging to Christ!

that you may love the Lord your God, listen to his voice,
and hold fast to him. For the Lord is your life...
Deuteronomy 30:20
(cf. Colossians 3:4)

We love him, because he first loved us.
1 John 4:19, KJV

Appendix A
<u>Understanding</u>
(King James Version)

1. God's

Great *is* our Lord, and of great power: his **understanding** *is* infinite. Psalms 147:5

Hast thou not known? hast thou not heard, *that* the everlasting God, the LORD, the Creator of the ends of the earth, fainteth not, neither is weary? *there is* no searching of his **understanding.**
Isaiah 40:28

And all that heard him were astonished at his **understanding** and answers.
Luke 2:47

And the spirit of the LORD shall rest upon him, the spirit of wisdom and **understanding,** the spirit of counsel and might, the spirit of knowledge and of the fear of the LORD; And shall make him of quick **understanding** in the fear of the LORD: and he shall not judge after the sight of his eyes, neither reprove after the hearing of his ears:
Isaiah 11:2-3

2. Lacking

For they *are* a nation void of counsel, neither *is there any* **understanding** in them.
Deuteronomy 32:28

Be ye not as the horse, *or* as the mule, *which* have no **understanding:** whose mouth must be held in with bit and bridle, lest they come near unto thee.
Psalms 32:9

But whoso committeth adultery with a woman lacketh **understanding:** *he that doeth it destroyeth his own soul.*
Proverbs 6:32

And beheld among the simple ones, I discerned among the youths, a young man void of **understanding**
Proverbs 7:7

The man that wandereth out of the way of **understanding** shall remain in the congregation of the dead.
Proverbs 21:16

I went by the field of the slothful, and by the vineyard of the man void of **understanding;** And, lo, it was all grown over with thorns, and nettles had covered the face thereof, and the stone wall thereof was broken down.
Proverbs 24:30-31

When the boughs thereof are withered, they shall be broken off: the women come, *and* set them on fire: for it *is* a people of no **understanding:** therefore he that made them will not have mercy on them, and he that formed them will shew them no favour.

Isaiah 27:11

And none considereth in his heart, neither *is* *there* knowledge nor **understanding** to say, I have burned part of it in the fire; yea, also I have baked bread upon the coals thereof; I have roasted flesh, and eaten *it*: and shall I make the residue thereof an abomination? shall I fall down to the stock of a tree?
Isaiah 44:19

Hear now this, O foolish people, and without **understanding;** which have eyes, and see not; which have ears, and hear not:
Jeremiah 5:21

And now they sin more and more, and have made them molten images of their silver, *and* idols according to their own **understanding,** all of it the work of the craftsmen: they say of them, Let the men that sacrifice kiss the calves.
Hosea 13:2

And Jesus said, Are ye also yet without **understanding?**
Matthew 15:16

Without **understanding,** covenantbreakers, without natural affection, implacable, unmerciful:
Romans 1:31

Having the **understanding** darkened, being alienated from the life of God through the ignorance that is in them, because of the blindness of their heart:
Ephesians 4:18

3. Sought after

I *am* thy servant; give me **understanding,** that I may know thy testimonies.
Psalms 119:125

The righteousness of thy testimonies *is* everlasting: give me **understanding,** and I shall live.   Psalms 119:144
Let my cry come near before thee, O LORD: give me **understanding** according to thy word.
Psalms 119:169

So that thou incline thine ear unto wisdom, *and* apply thine heart to **understanding;**
Proverbs 2:2

Yea, if thou criest after knowledge, *and* liftest up thy voice for **understanding;**
Proverbs 2:3

Hear, ye children, the instruction of a father, and attend to know **understanding.**
 Proverbs 4:1

Get wisdom, get **understanding:** forget *it* not; neither decline from the words of my mouth.
Proverbs 4:5

Wisdom *is* the principal thing; *therefore* get wisdom: and with all thy getting get **understanding.**
Proverbs 4:7

My son, attend unto my wisdom, *and* bow thine ear to my **understanding:**
Proverbs 5:1

Say unto wisdom, Thou *art* my sister; and call **understanding** *thy* kinswoman:
Proverbs 7:4

O ye simple, understand wisdom: and, ye fools, be ye of an **understanding** heart.
Proverbs 8:5
Forsake the foolish, and live; and go in the way of **understanding.**
Proverbs 9:6

He that refuseth instruction despiseth his own soul: but he that heareth reproof getteth **understanding.**
Proverbs 15:32

Buy the truth, and sell *it* not; *also* wisdom, and instruction, and **understanding.**
Proverbs 23:23

4. Source

And unto man he said, Behold, the fear of the Lord, that *is* wisdom; and to depart from evil *is* **understanding.**
Job 28:28

But *there is* a spirit in man: and the inspiration of the Almighty giveth them **understanding.**
Job 32:8

The fear of the LORD *is* the beginning of wisdom: a good **understanding** have all they that do *his* *commandments*: his praise endureth for ever.
Psalms 111:10

Through thy precepts I get **understanding:** therefore I hate every false way.
Psalms 119:104

The entrance of thy words giveth light; it giveth **understanding** unto the simple.
Psalms 119:130
For the LORD giveth wisdom: out of his mouth *cometh* knowledge and **understanding.**
Proverbs 2:6

Then opened he their **understanding,** that they might understand the scriptures,
Luke 24:45

Consider what I say; and the Lord give thee **understanding** in all things.
2 Timothy 2:7

And we know that the Son of God is come, and hath given us an **understanding,** that we may know him that is true, and we are in him that is true, *even* in his Son Jesus Christ. This is the true God, and eternal life.
1 John 5:20

5. Results

A wise *man* will hear, and will increase learning; and a man of **understanding** shall attain unto wise counsels:
Proverbs 1:5

So that thou incline thine ear unto wisdom, *and* apply thine heart to **understanding;** Yea, if thou criest after knowledge, *and* liftest up thy voice for **understanding;** If thou seekest her as silver, and searchest for her as for hid treasures; Then shalt thou understand the fear of the LORD, and find the knowledge of God.
Proverbs 2:2-5

Discretion shall preserve thee, **understanding** shall keep thee:
 Proverbs 2:11
Trust in the LORD with all thine heart; and lean not unto thine own **understanding.**
Proverbs 3:5

Good **understanding** giveth favour: but the way of transgressors *is* hard.
Proverbs 13:15

Wisdom resteth in the heart of him that hath **understanding:** but *that which is* in the midst of fools is made known.
Proverbs 14:33

How much better *is it* to get wisdom than gold! and to get **understanding** rather to be chosen than silver!
Proverbs 16:16

He that getteth wisdom loveth his own soul: he that keepeth **understanding** shall find good.
Proverbs 19:8

Through wisdom is an house builded; and by **understanding** it is established:
Proverbs 24:3

They also that erred in spirit shall come to **understanding,** and they that murmured shall learn doctrine.
Isaiah 29:24

And at the end of the days I Nebuchadnezzar lifted up mine eyes unto heaven, and mine **understanding** returned unto me, and I blessed the most High, and I praised and honoured him that liveth for ever, whose dominion *is* an everlasting dominion, and his kingdom *is* from generation to generation:
Daniel 4:3
And to love him with all the heart, and with all the **understanding,** and with all the soul, and with all the strength, and to love *his* neighbour as himself, is more than all whole burnt offerings and sacrifices.
Mark 12:33

The eyes of your **understanding** being enlightened; that ye may know what is the hope of his calling, and what the riches of the glory of his inheritance in the saints,
Ephesians 1:18

Wherefore be ye not unwise, but **understanding** what the will of the Lord *is.*
Ephesians 5:17

For this cause we also, since the day we heard *it,* do not cease to pray for you, and to desire that ye might be filled with the knowledge of his will in all wisdom and spiritual **understanding;**
Colossians 1:9

Appendix B

What is an addiction/idolatry?

Addict- to devote or surrender (oneself) to something
habitually or excessively.
Merriam Webster Dictionary

**Arising out of our alienation from the Living God,
addiction is bondage to the rule of a substance, activity,
or state of mind, which then becomes the center of life,
defending itself from the truth, and leading to further
estrangement from God's kingdom.**
Edward T. Welch

The frenzy and barbarism of idolatry which stems from a
commitment to an erroneous, improper, and irreverent view
of the living and true God.
Gregory Madison

Who Is an Addict? (from Narcotics Anonymous)
**Most of us do not have to think twice about this question.
WE KNOW! Our whole life and thinking was centered
in drugs in one form or another -- the getting and using
and finding ways and means to get more. We lived to use
and used to live. Very simply, an addict is a man or
woman whose life is controlled by drugs.**

Idolatry is defined as "the worship of a physical object as a
god. "Idolatry is "immoderate" meaning there is no
moderation in the devotion to the object. The object has been
thought about, pursued, desired, and talked about
excessively. The object has become the center of the

universe in the idolater's eyes. The object has replaced Christ.
The Heart of Addiction Workbook- *Mark E. Shaw*

What is idolatry? (New City Catechism by *Tim Keller and Sam Shammas*)
Idolatry is trusting in created things rather than the Creator for our hope and happiness, significance and security.

What is an idol? It is anything more important to you than God, anything that absorbs your heart and imagination more than God, anything you seek to give you what only God can give. A counterfeit god is anything so central and essential to your life that, should you lose it, your life would feel hardly worth living. An idol has such a controlling position I your heart that you can spend most of your passion and energy, your emotional and financial resources, on it without a second thought... An idol is whatever you look at and say, in your heart of hearts, "If I have that, then I'll feel my life has meaning, then I'll know I have value, then I'll feel significant and secure."
Tim Keller— "Counterfeit Gods"

We Become What We Worship
G.K. Beale

At the root, then, all idolatry is human rejection of the Goodness of God and the finality of God's authority.

What is sobriety?

To be sober not only means to be abstinent or not intoxicated. Being sober, also, means to be serious, solemn, devoid of frivolity, wise, moderate and sane (or rational). In a biblical sense the word sober means to be discreet, watchful, of a sound mind, humble and disciplined. Sobriety compels us to think about what really matters. It can be said that Jesus Christ was and always will be the sanest person that ever lives. Perhaps, this is why He said to seek first the kingdom of God and His righteousness, and all of our other needs would be met (Matthew 6:33).

After taking a long look at what life is about, Solomon (who is said to be the wisest man that ever lived) tells us of the importance of putting God first. In Ecclesiastes 12:13 he said, "Let us hear the conclusion of the whole matter: Fear God and keep his commandments; for this is the whole duty of man".

Clean and Sober for the Right Reasons

Staying away from drugs and alcohol is not easy for a person who has a history of substance abuse. It's a matter of reforming values. At best abstinence is achieved by maintaining an active relationship with Jesus Christ (who is called the wisdom and power of God, 1 Cor. 1:24). The worst thing a person can do is to abstain from an addiction for *the wrong motives. First of all, if a person doesn't have the right motives for abstaining, then he is "out of sync" with God. Secondly, when a person does not have the right motives in abstaining from his addiction, then he lives by his own standards (he makes the rules). Thirdly, when people don't abstain with the right motives, then they are more likely to return to their addiction or turn to another addiction. The highest motive for abstaining is to show our reverence towards God.

Improper motives are all centered upon the person. Improper motives could be based on trying to gain a good reputation, earn wealth, getting the family back, to please the boss, etc. These *lesser* motives may appear to be okay (on the surface), but let us not be deceived; they are self-centered motives just the same. I believe that those who said that the road to abstinence is a "selfish program" really were trying to say that it's a *personal* program. As Philippians 2:12b says, "work out your own salvation with fear and trembling..." (reverence for God).

When a person is not abstaining from an addiction (not just substance abuse) for the right reason, there is no spirituality. Many will claim to work a "spiritual program" when (in actuality) it's just a psychological program with a bunch of spiritual jargon. To work a spiritual program we must be connected with God. We must be "in sync" with God and striving to surrender ourselves to him fully. We must realize that we will give an account to God. We must be willing to embrace godly principles. James 3:13-17 helps us to recognize the difference between a selfish program and a spiritual program.

> *Who is wise and understanding among you? Let him show it by his good life, by deeds done in the humility that comes from wisdom. But if you harbor bitter envy and selfish ambition in your hearts, do not boast about it or deny the truth. Such "wisdom" does not come down from heaven but is earthly, unspiritual, of the devil. For where you have envy and selfish ambition, there you find disorder and every evil practice. But the wisdom that comes from heaven is first of all pure; then peace-loving,*

considerate, submissive, full of mercy and good fruit, impartial and sincere.

What is your main reason for not drinking and/or drugging? Is it because it was ruining your life? Or was it because you recognized it as being wrong in the sight of God? I'm not saying that we should not be concerned about the impact of addiction on our personal lives, but if we do not abstain out of reverence for God, then our motives will be less than pure. It's really a question of what we value. Do we value God, or do we value family, possessions or reputation more? Jesus Christ explained to His followers that there is a decision they all had to make. In Matthew 10: 37-39 He said, "He who loves father or mother more than me is not worthy of me. And he who loves son or daughter more than me is not worthy of me. And he who does not take his cross and follow after me is not worthy of me. He who finds his life will lose it, and he who loses his life for my sake will find it."

To abstain from an addiction out of love and respect for God is an act of worship. In this we say, "God, you are worthy of my abstinence." Here's where we are "in sync" with God. Here we have opened ourselves to God's wisdom and direction. We agree to live by His standards. When we don't have the right motives for staying clean and sober, we are living according to our own standards. If my sobriety is not based on the principles of God, then I am living by my own standards. I determine what's right and what's wrong. Who's to say that I might not change my mind about whether it's right engage in an addiction? What's to keep me from doing *other* things that are not in my best interest or the interest of others (as well as displeasing to God)? We, in effect, design our own program. At best, we possess a *form* of godliness. This type of sobriety is of a lower nature (as well as being displeasing to God). Here we are leaning on our own understanding. In doing so we may be inclined to leave so many other issues unaddressed.

When we are not staying clean and sober as an act of worship, we are more likely to return to our addiction, or turn to some other addiction. The reason that people who are abstinent for the wrong reasons are likely to return to substance abuse is because they lack the wisdom of God. We can take courage in the fact that God recognizes and rewards those who are seeking a higher degree of reverence (Ps. 86:11). When we do not abstain out of reverence for God, as quiet as it's kept, this is sowing to the flesh. Ultimately, we are being irreverent towards God in one degree or another.

Conclusion

Some may not agree, but in my opinion, to abstain from an addiction for the wrong reason (s) is just as bad (if not worse) than indulgence.

1. A false sense of security
2. Ignoring God
3. Lack of quality sobriety
4. Based on fear – of losing family, friends, job...

This, also, pertains to the counselee's relationship to God. "Much change that is offered today in counseling—even in the Name of Christ—is sub-Christian. Aimed at little more than making counselees happier, it neglects the basic reason why a believer must change to please God. As if God's glory were of secondary importance, His Name's sake is omitted from the picture, out of deference to better health or a more smoothly running marriage. Such considerations, not wrong in themselves, are quite wrong when they are not subordinated to the greater purpose of pleasing and honoring God."

How to Help People Change- Jay Adams

A Deeper Study of the Word of God on Addictions
By Gregory Madison

1. A matter of reverence for God
2. Builds faith in God
a. Addicts tend to have a small view of God
(1) God is good
(2) God offer's forgiveness
(3) God has all power
b. Being on one accord with God/providing communion with God
(1) God speaks
(2) Grounds for praying according to the will of God

3. Dispels deception and error
a. About God
b. About oneself
c. About addiction/sin

4. Provides an alternative to the addiction
a. Proper motives for sobriety
b. Putting on Christ

5. Teaches how to help others
a. Provides wisdom
b. The sword of the Spirit (also, James 5:19f.)

6. The irreverence of turning to other sources (turning from God)

a. We are saying that God doesn't know enough- He's a fool
b. We are saying God doesn't care enough- He is evil and can't be trusted
c. We are saying God doesn't have enough power- He is weak and sorry
d. We are saying that we don't care what God has to say- I've got all the answers
e. We are saying that we don't mind on taking a chance of being deceived
f. We are saying that God doesn't have the right to tell me what to do

Appendix C

The idols in the Bible vs. the idols of today

There are similarities between the way idols affected Biblical characters and how addictions affect people. 2 Chronicles 28:23 gives one example. The verse records how King Ahaz "sought help from idols." People seek all kinds of help from addictions. They look for courage, rejuvenation, and a number of other things. The verse goes onto say that the idols were the ruin of King Ahaz and all of Israel. Addictions have been the ruin of many. Ahaz should have sought help from the Lord, as those who are bond to addictions should.

Many of the phrases used in Deuteronomy 32:15-29 (which describes Israel's idolatry) correspond with the experience people go through as they engage in addiction. Verse 15 says that Jeshurun [Israel] grew fat, thick and sleek. Many who engage in addictions have tremendous resources at their disposal. Often, it costs a lot of money to supply a habit, and those who are not "fat" financially make up for it through methods that are often immoral and corrupt. Jeshurun forsook God. How many people who are bond to addictions are truly seeking God? We are also told that Israel lightly esteemed the rock of His salvation. God was not very important to them. They did not have a high regard for God. They angered God with their detestable idols (verse 17, NIV). The idols within the world of addictions are so detestable that it is hard to see how men are created in the image of God. This is because the actions of that person indicate a life that is totally given to self-fulfillment and self-gratification, while God is love.

Israel sacrificed to gods just as people sacrifice to various addictions. Verse 18 says that they were unmindful of God. We tend to center our thoughts on the things that are most important to us. When a person's life is centered upon an addiction, their thoughts are certainly not centered around God. We are also told that the Israelites were rejected by God and that He hid His face from them (verse 19f, NIV).

People who are bond to addictions experience separation from God. The Israelites were called a perverse and crooked generation. In this case, perverse means distorted or false. So distorted is the addict, that he sees his addiction as being of more importance than his welfare or the welfare of others. So false is the thinking of those who cling to addictions, that they try to find peace and fulfillment in the addiction. Israel's idols were foolish. The NIV says that their idols were worthless. These ideas also apply to addictions.

In verse 23, God said that He would heap disasters (NAS, misfortunes) upon that generation of Israelites. The lives of many addicts have been full of disaster. The Lord also said that the Israelites would be wasted with hunger. Many addicts become malnourished in the preoccupation of feeding their habits. Verse 25 talks about the Israelites going against "the sword" and being defeated. The life of the addict is often met by physical confrontation through one source or another.

The Lord said that He would make the memory of that generation to cease from among men. As relationships are severed through addictions, the addict becomes a forgotten person. Verses 28-29 explain how the Israelites were a nation without sense (NIV; NAS says, "lacking counsel"). We are also told that they had no understanding. People who engage in addictions sometimes act as though they have no sense; they are sometimes hard to reason with and display no understanding whatsoever. Psalm 32:9a says to be not as the horse or the mule, which have no understanding. How ironic it is that some people refer to themselves as party animals!

Warnings Against Idolatry

Take careful heed to yourselves, for you saw no form when the Lord spoke to you at Horeb out of the midst of the fire, lest you act corruptly and make for yourselves a carved image in the form of any figure. Deut. 4:15-16a

Take heed to yourselves, lest you forget the covenant of the Lord your God which He made with you, and make for yourselves a carved image in the form of anything which the Lord your God has forbidden you. Deut. 4:23

When you beget children and grandchildren and have grown old in the land, and act corruptly and make a carved image in the form of anything, and do evil in the sight of the Lord your God to provoke Him to anger. Deut.4:25

Then it shall be, if you by any means forget the Lord your God, and follow other gods, and serve them and worship them, I testify against you this day that you shall surely perish.
Deut. 8:19

Take heed to yourselves, lest your heart be deceived, and you turn aside and serve other gods and worship them, lest the Lord's anger be aroused against you, and He shut up the heavens so that there be no rain, and the land yield no produce, and you perish quickly from the good land which the Lord is giving you.
Deut. 11:16-17

Take heed to yourself that you are not ensnared to follow them, after they are destroyed from before you, and that you do not inquire after their gods, saying, 'How did these nations serve their gods? I also will do likewise.
Deut. 12:30

But if you turn away and forsake My statutes and My commandments which I have set before you, and go and serve other gods, and worship them, then I will uproot them from My land which I have given them; and this house which I have sanctified for My name I will cast out of My sight, and will make it a proverb and a byword among all peoples. And as for this house, which is exalted, everyone who passes by it will be astonished and say, 'Why has the Lord done thus to this land and this house?' Then they will answer, 'Because they forsook the Lord God of their

fathers, who brought them out of the land of Egypt, and embraced other gods, and worshiped them and served them; therefore He has brought all this calamity on them.
2 Chron. 7:19-22

Do not go after other gods to serve them and worship them, and do not provoke Me to anger with the works of your hands; and I will not harm you.
Jer. 25:6

Therefore, my beloved, flee from idolatry.
1 Corinthians 10:14

Therefore put to death your members which are on the earth: fornication, uncleanness, passion, evil desire, and covetousness, which is idolatry.
Col. 3:5

God's Judgment Against Idolatry

Now therefore, go, lead the people to the place of which I have spoken to you. Behold, My Angel shall go before you. Nevertheless, in the day when I visit for punishment, I will visit punishment upon them for their sin." So the Lord plagued the people because of what they did with the calf which Aaron made.
Exodus 32:34-35

But if your heart turns away so that you do not hear, and are drawn away, and worship other gods and serve them, I announce to you today that you shall surely perish; you shall not prolong your days in the land which you cross over the Jordan to go in and possess. I call heaven and earth as witnesses today against you, that I have set before you life and death, blessing and cursing; therefore choose life, that both you and your descendants may live
Deut. 30:17-19

And the Lord said to Moses: "Behold, you will rest with your fathers; and this people will rise and play the harlot with the gods of the foreigners of the land, where they go to be among them, and they will forsake Me and break My covenant which I have made with them. Then My anger shall be aroused against them in that day, and I will forsake them, and I will hide My face from them, and they shall be devoured. And many evils and troubles shall befall them, so that they will say in that day, 'Have not these evils come upon us because our God is not among us?'
Deut. 31:16-17

For the Lord of hosts, who planted you, has pronounced doom against you for the evil of the house of Israel and of the house of Judah, which they have done against themselves to provoke Me to anger in offering incense to Baal.
Jer. 11:17

Then your altars shall be desolate, your incense altars shall be broken, and I will cast down your slain men before your idols. And I will lay the corpses of the children of Israel before their idols, and I will scatter your bones all around your altars. In all your dwelling places the cities shall be laid waste, and the high places shall be desolate, so that your altars may be laid waste and made desolate, your idols may be broken and made to cease, your incense altars may be cut down, and your works may be abolished. The slain shall fall in your midst, and you shall know that I am the Lord. "Yet I will leave a remnant, so that you may have some who escape the sword among the nations, when you are scattered through the countries. Then those of you who escape will remember Me among the nations where they are carried captive, because I was crushed by their adulterous heart which has departed from Me, and by their eyes which play the harlot after their idols; they will loathe themselves for the evils which they committed in all their abominations. And they shall know that I am the Lord; I have not said in vain that I would bring this calamity upon them."'Thus says the Lord God: "Pound your fists and stamp your feet, and say, 'Alas, for all the evil abominations of the house of Israel! For

they shall fall by the sword, by famine, and by pestilence. He who is far off shall die by the pestilence, he who is near shall fall by the sword, and he who remains and is besieged shall die by the famine. Thus will I spend My fury upon them.

Ezek. 6:4-12

"I will sweep away everything from the face of the earth," declares the Lord. "I will sweep away both men and animals; I will sweep away the birds of the air and the fish of the sea. The wicked will have only heaps of rubble when I cut off man from the face of the earth," declares the Lord. "I will stretch out my hand against Judah and against all who live in Jerusalem. I will cut off from this place every remnant of Baal, the names of the pagan and the idolatrous priests-- those who bow down on the roofs to worship the starry host, those who bow down and swear by the Lord and who also swear by Molech, those who turn back from following the Lord and neither seek the Lord nor inquire of him.
Zeph. 1:2-6

Futility and Deceit of Idolatry

Do not bring a detestable thing into your house or you, like it, will be set apart for destruction. Utterly abhor and detest it, for it is set apart for destruction.
Deut. 7:26

"I have not made trouble for Israel," Elijah replied. "But you and your father's family have. You have abandoned the Lord's commands and have followed the Baals.
I Kings 18:18

He offered sacrifices to the gods of Damascus, who had defeated him; for he thought, "Since the gods of the kings of Aram have helped them, I will sacrifice

to them so they will help me." But they were his downfall and the downfall of all Israel.
2 Chron. 28:23

They worshiped their idols, which became a snare to them.
Ps.106:36

Bring in your idols to tell us what is going to happen. Tell us what the former things were, so that we may consider them and know their final outcome. Or declare to us the things to come, tell us what the future holds, so we may know that you are gods. Do something, whether good or bad, so that we will be dismayed and filled with fear. But you are less than nothing and your works are utterly worthless; he who chooses you is detestable... I look but there is no one-- no one among them to give counsel, no one to give answer when I ask them. See, they are all false! Their deeds amount to nothing; their images are but wind and confusion.
Isa. 41:22-24,28, 29

All who make idols are nothing, and the things they treasure are worthless. Those who would speak up for them are blind; they are ignorant, to their own shame. Who shapes a god and casts an idol, which can profit him nothing?... He feeds on ashes, a deluded heart misleads him; he cannot save himself, or say, "Is not this thing in my right hand a lie?"
Isa. 44: 9-10, 20

The sorrows of those will increase who run after other gods.
Ps. 16:4a

118

All the makers of idols will be put to shame and disgraced; they will go off into disgrace together. Gather together and come; assemble, you fugitives from the nations. Ignorant are those who carry about idols of wood, who pray to gods that cannot save.
Isa. 45:16, 20

Bel bows down, Nebo stoops low; their idols are borne by beasts of burden. The images that are carried about are burdensome, a burden for the weary.
Isa. 46:1

Everyone is senseless and without knowledge; every goldsmith is shamed by his idols. His images are a fraud; they have no breath in them. They are worthless, the objects of mockery; when their judgment comes, they will perish.
Jer. 10:14-15

For they shall eat, and not have enough: they shall commit whoredom, and shall not increase: because they have left off to take heed to the LORD. Whoredom and wine and new wine take away the heart. My people ask counsel at their stocks, and their staff declareth unto them: for the spirit of whoredoms hath caused them to err, and they have gone a whoring from under their God.
Hos. 4:10-12

They that observe lying vanities forsake their own mercy.
Jon. 2:8

Of what value is an idol, since a man has carved it? Or an image that teaches lies? For he who makes it trusts in his own creation; he makes idols that cannot speak. Woe to him who says to wood, 'Come to life!' Or to lifeless stone, 'Wake up!' Can it give guidance? It is covered with gold and silver; there is no breath in it. But the Lord is in his holy temple; let all the earth be silent before him.
Hab. 2:18-20

And what agreement hath the temple of God with idols?
2 Cor. 6:16a

Examples of Idolatry

Yet they would not listen to their judges but prostituted themselves to other gods and worshiped them. Unlike their fathers, they quickly turned from the way in which their fathers had walked, the way of obedience to the Lord's commands. Whenever the Lord raised up a judge for them, he was with the judge and saved them out of the hands of their enemies as long as the judge lived; for the Lord had compassion on them as they groaned under those who oppressed and afflicted them. But when the judge died, the people returned to ways even more corrupt than those of their fathers, following other gods and serving and worshiping them. They refused to give up their evil practices and stubborn ways.
Judges 2:17-19

Go, tell Jeroboam that this is what the Lord, the God of Israel, says... You have done more evil than all
120

who lived before you. You have made for yourself other gods, idols made of metal; you have provoked me to anger and thrust me behind your back.
1 Kings 14:7a, 9

They sacrificed their sons and daughters in the fire. They practiced divination and sorcery and sold themselves to do evil in the eyes of the Lord, provoking him to anger.
2 Kings 17:17

As a thief is disgraced when he is caught, so the house of Israel is disgraced-- they, their kings and their officials, their priests and their prophets. They say to wood, 'You are my father,' and to stone, 'You gave me birth.' They have turned their backs to me and not their faces; yet when they are in trouble, they say, 'Come and save us!' Where then are the gods you made for yourselves? Let them come if they can save you when you are in trouble! For you have as many gods as you have towns, O Judah.
Jer. 2:26-28

These wicked people, who refuse to listen to my words, who follow the stubbornness of their hearts and go after other gods to serve and worship them, will be like this belt--completely useless!
Jer. 13:10

Because of all your detestable idols, I will do to you what I have never done before and will never do again. Therefore in your midst fathers will eat their children, and children will eat their fathers. I will inflict punishment on you and will scatter all your survivors to the winds. Therefore as surely as I live, declares the Sovereign Lord, because you have defiled my sanctuary with all your vile images and detestable practices, I myself will withdraw my favor; I will not look on you with pity or spare you. A third of your people will die of the plague or perish by famine inside you; a third will fall by the sword outside your walls; and a third I will scatter to the winds and pursue with drawn sword. "Then my anger will cease and my wrath against them will subside, and I will be avenged. And when I have spent my wrath upon them, they will know that I the Lord have spoken in my zeal. "I will make you a ruin and a reproach among the nations around you, in the sight of all who pass by.

Ezek. 5:9-14

When you offer your gifts--the sacrifice of your sons in the fire--you continue to defile yourselves with all your idols to this day. Am I to let you inquire of me, O house of Israel? As surely as I live, declares the Sovereign Lord, I will not let you inquire of me.

Ezek. 20:31

When Ephraim spoke, men trembled; he was exalted in Israel. But he became guilty of Baal worship and died. Now they sin more and more; they make idols for themselves from their silver, cleverly fashioned images, all of them the work of craftsmen. It is said of these people, "They offer human sacrifice and kiss the calf-idols." Therefore they will be like the morning mist, like the early dew that disappears, like chaff swirling from a threshing floor, like smoke escaping through a window. "But I am the Lord your

God, who brought you out of Egypt. You shall acknowledge no God but me, no Savior except me.
Hosea 13:1-4

While Paul was waiting for them in Athens, he was greatly distressed to see that the city was full of idols.

Acts 17:16

Repentance: Turning from Idolatry

So Jacob said to his household and to all who were with him, "Get rid of the foreign gods you have with you, and purify yourselves and change your clothes".

Gen. 35:2

Do not bow down before their gods or worship them or follow their practices. You must demolish them and break their sacred stones to pieces.
Ex. 23:24
"Now fear the Lord and serve him with all faithfulness. Throw away the gods your forefathers worshiped beyond the River and in Egypt, and serve the Lord. "Now then," said Joshua, "throw away the foreign gods that are among you and yield your hearts to the Lord, the God of Israel."
Jos. 24:14, 23

And Samuel said to the whole house of Israel, "If you are returning to the Lord with all your hearts, then rid yourselves of the foreign gods and the Ashtoreths

and commit yourselves to the Lord and serve him only, and he will deliver you out of the hand of the Philistines." So the Israelites put away their Baals and Ashtoreths, and served the Lord only. Then Samuel said, "Assemble all Israel at Mizpah and I will intercede with the Lord for you." When they had assembled at Mizpah, they drew water and poured it out before the Lord. On that day they fasted and there they confessed, "We have sinned against the Lord."
1 Sam. 7:3-6

Asa did what was good and right in the eyes of the Lord his God. He removed the foreign altars and the high places, smashed the sacred stones and cut down the Asherah poles. He commanded Judah to seek the Lord, the God of their fathers, and to obey his laws and commands. He removed the high places and incense altars in every town in Judah, and the kingdom was at peace under him. He built up the fortified cities of Judah, since the land was at peace. No one was at war with him during those years, for the Lord gave him rest.
2 Chron. 14:2-6

When Asa heard these words and the prophecy of Azariah son of Oded the prophet, he took courage. He removed the detestable idols from the whole land of Judah and Benjamin and from the towns he had captured in the hills of Ephraim He repaired the altar of the Lord that was in front of the portico of the Lord's temple.
2 Chron. 15:8

His heart was devoted to the ways of the Lord;
furthermore, he removed the high places and the
Asherah poles from Judah.
2 Chron. 17:6

Josiah removed all the detestable idols from all the
territory belonging to the Israelites, and he had all
who were present in Israel serve the Lord their God.
As long as he lived, they did not fail to follow the
Lord, the God of their fathers
2 Chron. 34;33

Elijah went before the people and said, "How long
will you waver between two opinions? If the Lord is
God, follow him; but if Baal is God, follow him."
But the people said nothing.
1 Kings 18:21

"Therefore say to the house of Israel, 'This is what
the Sovereign Lord says: Repent! Turn from your
idols and renounce all your detestable practices!'"
Ezek. 14:6

And I said to them, "Each of you, get rid of the vile
images you have set your eyes on, and do not defile
yourselves with the idols of Egypt. I am the Lord
your God."
Ezek. 20:7

Many of those who believed now came and openly
confessed their evil deeds. A number who had
practiced sorcery brought their scrolls together and
burned them publicly. When they calculated the
value of the scrolls, the total came to fifty thousand

drachmas. In this way the word of the Lord spread widely and grew in power. Acts 19:18-20

Therefore, my dear friends, flee from idolatry.
1 Cor. 10:14

for they themselves report what kind of reception you gave us. They tell how you turned to God from idols to serve the living and true God.
1 Thes. 1:9

Appendix D

The Fear of the Lord

Essential reverence

Showing reverence for God is an essential element for remaining abstinent of an addiction because it gives us the wisdom we need to combat all of the fleshly desires that would draw us towards addictions and away from God. Proverbs 9:10 says that the fear of the Lord (reverence for God) is the beginning of wisdom. If we would take the time to consider the Lord in all our endeavors, if we would seek Him out in all our affairs, He will show us what to do.

Jesus Christ is called "the wisdom and the power of God" (1 Cor. 1:24). As we draw near to Christ, He will draw closer to us, then, we will be able to avoid the snares of the devil. Many of the situations that used to baffle us will become *eliminated*. It is best that a person's primary reason for abstaining from an addiction is out of reverence for God. This indicates a true and humble desire to change, which is not only pleasing to God, but advantageous to us.

When we abstain out of love and respect for God, we begin to really live. We become whole, because we are faced the reality of God's presence each and every day. We become responsible individuals, possessing a degree of integrity, because they are mindful of their obligation to God. An understanding of what God is like illuminates our minds. Ultimately, and in addition, we are blessed with wisdom because we have decided to side with Jesus Christ (on His terms).

A definition for the fear of the Lord:

The Hebrew word 'yare' is used in scripture when referring to fear. In the case of the fear of the Lord it is referring to reverence. Reverence, as defined by Vine's Expository Dictionary of Biblical Words, as "the recognition of the power and position of an individual revered and render Him proper respect. In this sense the word may imply submission to a proper ethical relationship to God". According to Jerry Bridges, the three elements of reverencing God are respect in recognition of His infinite worth and dignity, admiration of His glorious attributes, and amazement at His infinite love. The Thorndike-Barnhart Comprehensive Dictionary defines reverence as a feeling of deep respect mixed with wonder, awe, and love. Also, to revere means to love and respect deeply, honor greatly, show reverence for. Lastly, some of the ideas conveyed in the Strong Exhaustive Concordance and Dictionary for reverence are; **to prize (fix valuation upon), splendor, esteem (esp. of the highest degree), gaze, behold, take heed, bashfulness or modesty (towards God), honor, and enjoy.**

I. The Basis of our Reverence for God

A. God is worthy
  1. Because of Who He is
    a. To you it does appertain   Jeremiah 10:7
    b. Worthy is the Lamb   Revelations 5:12
    c. There is none like unto you   Jeremiah 10:7
    d. He is your praise   Deuteronomy 10:20-21
    e. He is your God   2 Corinthians 6:16
    f. Because He is the Father   2 Cor. 6:18
    g. The hand of the Lord is mighty   Josh. 4:24

    h. Because of His greatness   Psalm 96:4
    i. Our God is a consuming fire   Heb. 12:28
    j. Art to be feared   Psalm 76:7
    k. Ought to be feared   Psalm 76:11
    l. God is fearful in praises   Exodus 15:11
    m. His name is glorious and Wonderful
        Deut. 28:58
    n. He is just and true   Revelation 15:3-4
    o. He is holy   Revelation 15:4

2. Because of what He does
    a. Consider how great things he hath done
        1 Samuel 12:24
    b. Forgiving
        1 Kings 8:36,40
    c. Hearing prayer
        1 Kings 8:43
    d. Because of the goodness & prosperity
        Jer. 33:9
    e. which God gave

    f. God is working in you   Philippians 2:13
            a. To will His pleasure
            b. To do His good pleasure

B. As a covenant   2 Kings 17:35
C. Because of the reproach of the heathen   Neh. 5:9

D. It is required   Deuteronomy 10:12

E. A priority   1 Samuel 12:24

F. That they would not depart from God   Jer. 32:40

G. As a benefit
    a. They that honor me, I will honor   1 Sam. 2:30
    b. So their dwelling would not be cut off Zep. 3:7
    c. For our profit, to live   Heb. 12:9-10

d. Partakers of His holiness
e. For the good of them   Jer. 32:39
f. For the good of their children   Jer. 32:39

II. The Characteristics/ Components of our Reverence for God

   A.   So that you don't sin
          Exodus 20:20
   B.   All the days of your life
          Deut. 4:10
   C.   Love Him
          Deut. 10:12
   D.   Cleaving to Him
          Deut. 10:20
   E.   Greatly
          1 Kings 18:3
   F.   Sacrifice to Him
          2 Kings 17:36
   G.   Faithfully
          2 Chr.19:9
   H.   With a perfect heart
          2 Chr. 19:9
   I.   Walking in fear of the Lord
          Neh. 5:9
   J.   Worship   Psalms 5:7; 96:9
   K.   Praise Him   Psalms 22:23
   L.   Devoted to your fear
          Psalms 119:38
   M.   Sanctify the Lord   Isaiah 8:13
   N.   To receive instruction
          Zephaniah 3:7
   O.   Honoring the Lord   Isaiah 58:13
     1. Not doing your own ways
     2. Not finding your own pleasure

3. Not speaking your own words

P.   Sojourning in fear   1 Peter 1:17

Q.   Standing in awe   Psalms 33:8

III. Reverence as it is commanded in scripture

A. By Moses   Deuteronomy 31:12

B. By Joshua   Joshua 24:1,14

C. Jehoshaphat commanded the judges to
2 Chronicles 19:4-7
    a. Let it be upon you
    b. Take heed to do it
    c. Jehoshaphat charged them

D. By David   Psalm 2:11

E. By King Darius   Daniel 6:26

IV. A refusal to revere the Lord

A. Definition/description
    1. Despising the Lord   Proverbs 14:2
    2. Hardening your heart   Proverbs 28:14
    3. Their heart is far from me   Isaiah 29:13
    4. Not in thee   Jeremiah 2:19
      a. Exemplified through wickedness and
         backslidings
      b. Know and see
      c. It is an evil thing
      d. It is a bitter thing
      e. Have forsaken the Lord thy God
    5. Played the harlot   Jeremiah 3:8
    6. Not humbled (contrite, NAS)   Jer. 44:10
    7. They corrupted all their doing   Zep. 3:7

8. No fear of God before their eyes   Rom. 3:18
9. No respect towards God   Isaiah 22:11
10. This people honors me with their lips,
   but their hearts are far from me   Matt. 15:8
B. Did not choose the fear of the Lord   Pro. 1:29
   1. Simple ones
   2. Scorners
   3. Fools
   4. They hated knowledge
C. Consequences
   1.(Amalek) blotted out   Deuteronomy 25:19
   2. God shall afflict them   Psalm 55:19
   3. Years shortened   Proverbs. 10:27
   4. It shall not be well with them   Ecclesiastes 8:13
   5. His days are a shadow

V. Examples of reverence found in scripture

A. Abraham by not withholding Isaac

Gen. 20:11

B. Joseph   Genesis 42:18

C. Hanani   Nehemiah 7:2
   1. Given charge over Jerusalem
   2. A faithful man
   3. Feared God above many

D. Job   Job 1:8
   1. Perfect
   2. Upright
   3. Eschewed evil
   4. There was none like him in the earth
   5. Held fast his integrity   Job 2:3

E. Hezekiah   Jeremiah 26:19
    1. Besought the Lord
    2. The Lord repented of the evil He
pronounced against them

F. Levi was afraid before His name   Malachi 2:5-6
    1. The law of truth was in his mouth
    2. Iniquity was not found in his lips
    3. Walked with God in peace and equity
    4. Turned many away from iniquity

G. The centurion and those with him   Matthew 27:54
    1. Greatly
    2. Watching Jesus on the cross
    3. Upon seeing the earthquake
    4. Confessed that Jesus was the Son of God
H. Cornelius, the centurion   Acts 10:22
    1. A devout man
    2. Feared God with all his house
    3. Gave alms to the people
    4. Prayed to God always
    5. Of good report
    6. Others testified of his piety
I. A wise man fears   Proverbs 14:16
J. Nebuchadnezzer   Daniel 4:34
    1. Lifted up his eyes to heaven
    2. His understanding returned to him
    3. He blessed the most high
    4. He praised God
    5. He honored the Lord

VI. Proof of Reverence

A. By hearing God's word   Deuteronomy 4:10
B. Learning to   Deuteronomy 14:23

C. Walk in (all) His ways   Deut. 8:6; 10:12
D. Obeying His voice   Deut.13:4; 1Sam. 12:14
E. By hearkening   Psalm 34:18
F. Taught
G. By wisely considering his doing   Psalm 64:9
H. Delighting in His commandments   Ps. 112:1
I. Trusting in the Lord   Psalm 115:11
J. In all your ways acknowledge Him   Pro. 3:6
K. By not being wise in your own eyes   Pro. 3:7
L. Cleansing ourselves   2 Corinthians 7:1
   1. From all filthiness of the flesh
   2. From all filthiness of the spirit
   3. Perfecting holiness

VII. The Rewards of Reverencing God

A. There is harmony   Leviticus 25:36
B. Prosperity   Nehemiah 1:11
C. Those who do are honored   Psalm 15:4
D. Taught by God   Psalm 25:12
E. His soul shall dwell at ease   Psalm 25:13
F. The secret of the Lord is with them   Psalm 25:14
G. The goodness God has laid up for them is
     great   Psalm 31:19
H. The eye of the Lord is upon them   Psalm 33:18
I. Deliverance   Psalm 34:7
J. There is no want to them that fear Him
Psalm 34:9
K. A heritage   Psalm 61:5
L. His salvation is nigh to those who do   Psalm 85:9
M. His mercy is great towards those who do   Ps.103:11
N. The Lord pities those who do   Psalm 103:13
O. It is the beginning of wisdom   Ps.111:10;
Pro. 9:10

P. He is their help and their shield   Psalm 115:11
Q. You will eat the labor of your hands   Psalm 128:2
R. It shall be well with you
S. Your wife shall be a fruitful vine
T. He will hear their cry   Psalm 145:19
U. It is the beginning of knowledge   Proverbs 1:7
V. It will be health to your navel   Proverbs 3:8
W. It prolongs life   Proverbs 10:27
X. Strong confidence   Proverbs 14:26
Y. His children shall have a place of refuge
Z. It is a fountain   Proverbs 14:27
   1. of life
   2. to depart from the snares of death
AA. By it men depart from evil Proverbs 16:6
BB. When paired with humility it brings riches,
     honor, and life   Proverbs 22:4
CC. A woman who does shall be praised
    Proverbs 31:30
DD. He shall direct your paths   Proverbs 3:6
EE. Them that honor me I will honor
    1 Samuel 2:30

Is it Spiritual?

There is a new phenomenon, which is taking place where everybody wants to stand up and be counted as spiritual. Yet, many of the same individuals who claim to be "spiritual" lack one of the major qualities on which true spirituality is based. That one ingredient is reverence for God. In 2 Timothy 2:5 the apostle Paul said that there would be people in the last days who would have "a *form* of godliness but deny the power thereof". The apostle Paul was referring to people who are devoid of genuine reverence for the Lord Almighty.

Reverence for God has the capacity of turning people from sin. Where there is a disregard for God, people either ignore or seek to justify sin. Sometimes, people even deny sin, claiming that what the Bible says about a particular matter has no validity. They are saying that it's not a matter of what God says, everything is judged on the basis of what *I* think, how *I* feel; whether it will fulfill _my_ needs. This is the type of attitude that many have who *claim* to be spiritual.

If you look at the problems that plague our society, it can be noted that every one of these issues could be resolved through reverence for God on an individual or massive level. The issue, also, goes beyond just a change in action. We must consider our <u>motives</u> for wanting change. Why do we want to put an end to unnecessary pollution? Why should we save the whales? Why should people abstain from addictions? The list goes on…

If you were to present these questions to the general population, rarely would you hear someone say, "We should do so and so … out of reverence for God" (at least something of the sort). If you look at the majority of the programs that address substance abuse, you will notice that most of them say that the reason people should change is "for themselves". "You've got to do it for yourself", they say. Yet, the Word of God tells us that everything is to be done to glory of God… for the sake of Christ...

He died for all, that those who live should live no longer
for themselves, but for Him who died for them and rose
again.
2 Cor. 5:15

Furthermore, without the proper motives for doing what's right, people put limitations on the extent of their actions. Oh, we'll do what is required as long as it's to our advantage. Improper motives provide guidelines which are based on our own understanding (this we will tolerate, that we won't...) The point of it all is that there is nothing wrong with wanting a clean environment, the movement to put an end to drug abuse, saving the whales... Don't get me wrong, I'm not saying that we should not want a better world or a better life. However, if our reason for wanting these things is not first of all because of our reverence for God, we are lack an indispensable component.

As a result, we are prone to become selfish and more than often we make decisions which are ungodly, unhealthy and unwise. Contrary to what we may believe, though we are capable of making the noblest of decisions; though they may be ever so profitable, if they are not done with some sort of recognition for our Creator, these are ungodly decisions.

So, let us be careful about how we casually throw that word "spiritual" around. Let us keep in mind that reverence for the Almighty is at the heart of spirituality. Let us explore the motives behind our actions, and be sure to put our reverence for God on the top of the list, then and only then we can begin to call ourselves spiritual.

Appendix E

Actions

Reasons for abstinence

1. To avoid consequences
2. To find satisfaction in life
3. To honor God

Repentance

A. Leads to salvation (safety, salvaging...)
2 Cor. 7:10
B. Leaves no regret
C. Productive   2 Cor. 7:11
D. Earnestness
E. Eagerness
F. Indignation
G. Alarm
H. Longing
I. Concern
J. Readiness to see justice done
K. Produces fruit   Matt. 3:8
L. Produces spiritual health and wealth   Rev. 3:19
M. Requires vision
N. Based on truth (a response to the truth)
John 8:32
O. Assurance of truth comes before repentance
Acts 2:36-38
P. Gives direction
Q. Individual and personal

R. Involves confession
S. Intimacy with God
T. Honesty
U. Commanded to all by God   Acts 20:21
V. Repentance goes hand and hand with faith in Christ
W. Summoned by God's spokesmen
X. Grave and serious
Y. Offers promises
Z. Repentance is a serious matter
     (thus, it is sobering)
AA. Turning from ignorance to God
      Acts 3:17-20
BB. The Lord God takes joy in repentance
      Luke 15:7, 10, 24
CC. Necessary for forgiveness from God
      Acts 2:38

DD. God commands all people everywhere to
      repent Acts 17:30
EE. Repentance goes hand in hand with faith
      in Christ
FF. Our deeds prove our repentance
      Acts 26:20
GG. Repentance goes beyond knowledge
      (it is an experience with Christ)
HH. The Holy Spirit tells us what to
      do in order to repent   1 John 2:27-29
II. Repentance places us in the right position
      before God   Luke 5:8
JJ. Repentance <u>determines</u> our intimacy with
      the Almighty   2 Cor. 6:18-7:1
KK. Allows us to separate from the world
LL. Leads to sanctification
MM. It is a by-product of reverence
NN. Leads to purity

OO. Calls for priorities
PP. Restores order and manageability
QQ. Repentance is granted by God   2 Tim. 2:25

The Importance of Using Various Resources

My son, if you accept my words and store up my commands within you, turning your ear to wisdom and applying your heart to understanding, and if you call out for insight and cry aloud for understanding, and if you look for it as for silver and search for it as for hidden treasure, then you will understand the fear of the LORD and find the knowledge of God.   *Proverbs 2:1-4*

Where no counsel is, the people fall: but in the multitude of counselors there is safety.
Proverbs 11:14

1. God is not limited
2. The whole counsel of God   Acts 20:27
3. That which is profitable   Acts 20:20
4. Out of love for others
5. An appreciation of the body of Christ
          1 Cor. 12:21
6. Equipping ourselves and others to be more effective

(This could apply to any type of material that is of sound doctrine whether it be books, music, radio programs, tapes, etc.)

Bible based Resources on Addictions

BOOKS

1. Addictive Behavior by Edward Welch and Gary Shogren
2. The Heart of Addiction by Mark Shaw
3. Addictions: A Banquet in the Grave by Edward Welch
4. Running in Circles by Gary Shogren and Edward Welch
5. Counterfeit Gods by Timothy Keller
6. Gods at War by Kyle Idleman
7. There I Go Again: How to Keep from Falling for the Same Old Sin by Steven Mosley
8. How to How People Change by Jay Adams
9. The Doctrine of Repentance by Thomas Watson
10. It Ain't No Disease by Joyce Hovelsrud
11. A Repentant Heart by Dudley J. Delffs
12. The Sinfulness of Sin by Ralph Venning
13. Crosstalk by Mark Shaw
14. Pure Freedom: Breaking the Addiction to Pornography by Mike Cleveland
15. The Life Recovery Bible by Stephen Arterburn
16. Loving God With All My Heart by Julie Ackerman Link
17. How to Say No to a Stubborn Habit by Erwin W. Lutzer
18. Casting Down Idols, Through the Power of the Gospel by Pastor Michael R. Dixon

WORKBOOKS

19. The Heart of Addiction Workbook by Mark Shaw
20. Power to Choose by Mike S. O'Neil
21. Crossroads: A step by step guide away from addiction by Edward Welch

PAMPLETS AND ARTICLES

24. Just One More by Edward T. Welch

25. Clean: Seven Steps to Freedom by Richard and Susan Kollenberg
26. When a Man's Eye Wanders by Jeff Olson
27. When We Just Can't Stop by Tim Jackson and Jeff Olson
28. Articles by Gregory Madison

INTERNET

29. Turning to God from Idols Facebook page
30. Bible Verses Addictions Facebook page
31. High Sobriety Society Facebook page
32. The Fear of the Almighty Facebook page
33. Reverential Quest Facebook page
34. References of Reverence Facebook page
35. Redeemed Rebels: A Biblical Approach to Addiction, Part 1
    By Jeff Durbin
    https://chalcedon.edu/magazine/redeemed-rebels-a-biblical-
    approach-to-addiction-part-i

36. Redeemed Rebels: A Biblical Approach to Addiction, Part II, Bootleg Worship
    By Jeff Durbin
    https://chalcedon.edu/magazine/redeemed-rebels-a-biblical-approach-to-addiction-part-ii-bootleg-worship

37. Addictions and Idolatry
    by Edward Welch
    https://www.ligonier.org/learn/articles/addictions-and-idolatry/

38. Fight Addiction By Enjoying Jesus More
    https://www.youtube.com/watch?v=lei8gqTbWeY&feature=youtu.be

39. How to Fight Addiction in a Pornographic Culture
https://www.youtube.com/watch?v=hMEdy_rtp7o&feature=share
40. Unshackled.org

This is but a brief list. By the grace of God, the numbers are growing all of the time. Readers are advised to be very selective in your reading and purchasing. Though some other titles may be at least partial biblical, the approach man not be all that simplistic. Many of the books that I own and have scanned are not worthy of my recommendation.

Biblical Strategies for Dealing with Addictions

Common bond among Christian groups
1. We believe that addictions dishonor God
2. We recognize that addictions are useless
3. We believe that we are all vulnerable to addictions
4. We believe that true life is found in Christ alone
5. We believe that reverencing God is the key to sobriety
6. We believe that the motive for remaining abstinent should be to please God
7. We believe in the importance of building relationships with others

The Aim of the Christ-centered approach to Addictions
1. Bringing people to a saving knowledge of Christ
2. To encourage repentance of all that displeases God
3. To promote the joy and peace that is found in an active relationship with Christ
4. Fellowship with others believers (on various levels)
5. Allowing God to work through us

Signposts
When We Just Can't Stop by Tim Jackson

1. We admit we need help
2. We found that pain was not our enemy
3. We learned to accept responsibility for our own choices
4. We saw our need for mercy
5. We discovered that we have much to be thankful for
6. We discovered that surrender is a way of life
7. We devoted ourselves to helping others

The Process of Change
Addictions: A Banquet in the Grave by Edward T. Welch

Engage the battle- separate from the object of your affections

Turn to Christ and commit yourself to keep turning to Christ

Surround yourself with wise counselors- be a part of a church

Speak honestly- uncover the more subtle lies

Commit yourself to thinking God thoughts about addictions and wise living

Engage the battle to the lower level of the imagination

Delight in the fear of the Lord

Celebrate Recovery 8 Principles

1. Realize I'm not God
   I admit that I am powerless to control my tendency to do the wrong thing and my life is unmanageable

2. Earnestly believe that God exists, that I matter to Him, and that He has the power to help me recover
3. Consciously choose to commit all my life and will to Christ's care and control
4. Openly examine and confess my faults to God, to myself, and to someone I trust
5. Voluntarily submit to every change God wants to make in my life and humbly ask Him to remove my character defects
6. Evaluate all my relationships; offer forgiveness to those who have hurt me and make amends for harm I've done to others except when to do so would harm them or others
7. Reserve a daily time with God for self-examination, Bible reading, and prayer in order to know God and His will for my life and to gain the power to follow His will
8. Yield myself to be used to bring this Good News to others, both by my example and by my words

Reformer Unanimous' Principles

1. If God's against it so am I!
2. Every sin has its origin in our hearts.
3. It is easier to keep the heart clean than to clean it after it has been stained
4. We cannot fight a fleshly appetite by indulging in it.
5. Small compromises lead to great disasters.
6. Those who do not love the Lord will not help us serve the Lord.
7. Our sinful habits do hurt those who follow us.
8. It is not possible to fight a fleshly temptation with fleshly weapons.
9. We lose our freedom to choose when we give in to temptation.

Our consequences are inevitable and incalculable and up to God.
10. God balances guilt with blame. Accept the blame for your actions and God will remove the guilt.

Appendix F

Support Groups

Forming Christ-centered support groups

The first thing that we want to do in developing a support group is to adopt the same attitude that Paul had in regards to the church at Ephesus.

And how I kept back nothing that was profitable unto you
Acts 20:20a

We have been really, really blessed with some tremendous Bible-based resources on addictions over the last 20 years. There was a time that I would search bookstores and libraries for the resources that we are now endowed with (during my struggle with crack). I am very much encouraged over the fact that God is not a stingy Commander in Chief who orders His army to go forth against a mighty force with just a puny little arsenal. Nor is He a Provider who sends His servants out to feed the masses with just a smidgen of food. Use everything that is at your command!

With that being said, I would suggest a questionnaire for anyone who is interested in developing a Christ-centered group, as well as groups that are already in existence. These are the type of questions that need to be answered by all who are involved.

1. Does your group have a name?
2. How is the attendance?
3. What have you done to publicize your group?

4. What is the difference between Christ-centered groups and others?
5. Why would anyone choose a Christ-entered group over a regular group?
6. What type of resources does your group use?
7. Do you know of any other resources?
8. Do you know of any other groups?
9. What are the advantages of teaming up with other groups?
10. Are you completely satisfied with your group?
11. How's <u>your</u> life?
12. What are some of the strengths of your group?
13. What are some of your group's weaknesses?
14. What are some ways to make your group better?
15. Is it necessary for your group to make changes?
16. Does your group provide an outreach to its community?
17. How does Jesus make a difference in 'recovery'?
18. Do people have to turn to a prescribed pattern in order to overcome addiction?
19. Are you and/or those in your group willing to commit yourself to a city-wide effort?
20. Are you willing to help to get other groups started?

Here is a letter that I wrote to the Christ-centered groups in the Cleveland area some years ago which apply to each and every believer in Christ.

My dear friends,

I am writing this letter as an effort to share with you the vision which I believe the Lord has graciously set before us. As you know, where there is no vision the people perish (Proverbs 29:18). Let us take note of how evident this has been with the incidents that have taken place in our area over the last 6 months in relation to addicts. I don't know about you, but I am more and more convinced that people are in need of Christ in order to receive true sobriety. God has not given us a spirit of fear; but of power, and of love, and of a sound mind (2 Tim. 1:7). This is a promise to those who are in Christ. Another way to explain this is to look at the things that influence people. If an individual is not under the influence of Jesus Christ, then they are drunk with the world (and all it has to offer).

It is becoming more clear that the Church of the living God (in these United States, actually World Wide) is going to have to begin to become more active in presenting Christ as the means and source of sobriety. Please don't get me wrong, I am not trying to eliminate AA, NA, CA ...

God in His sovereignty uses people in that setting. God makes use of the 12 steps, also. But, is this the only way that God is able to rescue people? Who says that Bill W. (and the rest) knew the Bible better than anyone else? I am forever grateful to Frank Smith during the time he ministered out of Emmanuelle Baptist Church. This was the first time that I had seen anybody give a meeting on addictions directly out of the Bible. As someone who had become already familiar with the Bible; and had previously clung to every word that God would bring, those meetings were quite refreshing.

Yours in Christ,
Greg Madison

It was unfortunate that we were unable to form an association between the groups, but I would highly recommend this for every city. Often times, people will say that there are a lot of members at their church who need a support group, but are afraid of letting others in their church know that they have a problem. My response is to send them 'across town' to an associate group until they are comfortable enough to share in their home church.

My proposal for the groups in Cleveland was to name the association "The High Sobriety Society". The **purpose** of such an association is as follows;

1. To exalt Jesus Christ
2. To reinforce the message of sobriety in Christ
3. To invoke God's special blessing
4. To celebrate what God is doing
5. To bear one another's burden
6. To share ideas and resources
7. To provide fellowship
8. It increases the potential of forming other groups

With the following **declaration**;

We proclaim that sobriety is not just abstinence from addictions, but a total spiritual change, a renewed mind and changed heart. Being sober means the ability to make good choices and to use sound judgment. We exclaim that addictions are a matter of misplaced worship (the worshipping of idols). We insist that the highest form of sobriety known unto mankind is found in Jesus Christ and that anything that poses itself as sobriety, apart from Him, is only a façade.

Importance of Christ-centered support groups

1. A true and sure link to God
2. A true starting pointing i.e. offering forgiveness and salvation
3. The strength of the scriptures
4. Honest and effectual prayer
5. The closest fellowship possible
6. An act of worship

Last but not least, I suggest a schedule of all the Christ-centered groups within a particular area. The schedules are not only good for distributing among groups, but the following as well;

1. Vacation Bible schools
2. Hunger centers
3. 'Soup lines'
4. Community centers
5. Public housing buildings
6. Churches

Starting a group of your own

So, let's say that you have decided to start a group of your own but you can not decide on a format. I would strongly suggest any or all of the format which you will find below. First, let me give you a few things that need to be considered while you plan!

Question:
Why do we need a support group?

Answer:

To direct people to Christ.
Matthew 9:36
But when He saw the multitudes, He was moved with compassion for them, because they were like sheep having no shepherd.

Proverbs 24:11
Deliver those who are drawn toward death, and hold back those stumbling to the slaughter.

Question:
What is our main message?

Answer:

1. We proclaim that anything that we allow to take the place of God is an idol.
2. We pronounce that the main reason for abstinence is to give God glory.
3. We exclaim that the delight that is found in Christ surpasses the pleasures of the world.

Format

A. Prayer
B. Music
C. Readings
  1. Purpose
    TGFI* exists in order to provide and strengthen convictions concerning addictions, to provide fellowship and support to those who struggle with addictions, and to celebrate the freedom that is found in Jesus Christ.

  2. Declaration
    a. We proclaim that anything that we allow to take the place of God is an idol.
    b. We pronounce that the main reason for abstinence is to give God glory.
    c. We exclaim that the delight that is found in Christ surpasses the pleasures of the world.

  3. Rules
    a. Please do not comment if you have been under the influence of any mind or mood-altering substance in the last 24 hours.
    b. Please do not make any 'cross comments'.
    c. Please do not speak out of turn
    d. Please refrain from using profanity
    e. We ask that what is said in group remains confidential

* TGFI is my preference for a group name. It is a play on words. Rather than TGIF (Thank God it's Friday), we use TGFI (Turning to God from idols)

4. *Select* readings
   a. The nature of addiction**

   > Addiction is bondage to the rule of a substance, activity, or state of mind, which then becomes the center of life, defending itself from the truth so that even bad consequences don't bring repentance, and leading to further estrangement from God.

** Adopted from the writings of Edward T. Welch

   b. Principle of Turning to God from idols
      (1) Addiction are harmful and dishonor God.
      (2) God deserves to be honored and worshipped.
      (3) In and or ourselves, we are unable to resist temptation.
      (4) Only Jesus Christ can give us the power and the wisdom to live a godly life.
      (5) Our intimacy and reverence for God is more important than anything else.

5. Scripture reading (may vary)

1 Peter 2:11 (KJV)
Beloved, I beg you as sojourners and pilgrims, abstain from fleshly lusts which wage war against the soul.

2 Corinthians 5:15 (KJV)
And He died for all, that those who live should live no longer for themselves, but for Him who died for them and rose again.

Romans 13:11-14
And do this, knowing the time, that now it is high
time to awake out of sleep; for now our salvation is
nearer than when we first believed. The night is far
spent, the day is at hand. Therefore let us cast off the
works of darkness, and let us put on the armor of
light. Let us walk properly, as in the day, not in
revelry and drunkenness, not in lewdness and lust,
not in strife and envy. But put on the Lord Jesus
Christ, and make no provision for the flesh, to fulfill
its lusts.

6. Music
7. Introductions
    Who are you?
    Why are you here?

8. Discussion time (variety)
    a. Open discussion
    b. Speaker and comments
    c. Topic discussion
    d. Recording and discussion

9. Ending (Readings)
    a. Liabilities of addiction
        (1) Addiction is idolatry
        (2) Addiction is a poor use of energy
        (3) Addiction is a waste of time
        (4) Addiction is a waste of money
        (5) Addiction endangers your health
        (6) Addiction endangers your safety
        (7) Addiction endangers the safety of others
        (8) Addiction is non-productive
        (9) Addiction tears relationships apart

(10) Addiction is a bad example to others
(11) Addiction is the improper use of
      God's creation
(12) Addiction supports those who supply
      others with harmful substances

(13) Addiction reinforces a false sense of
      security
(14) Addiction is a stumbling block to
      others
(15) Addiction gives a bad testimony

b. 1 John 2:28-29
    And now, little children, abide in Him, that
    when He appears, we many have confidence
    and not be ashamed before Him at His
    coming. If you know that He is righteous,
    you know that everyone who practices
    righteousness is born of Him.

c. Prayer

** A special note on music-

The power of music unto the Lord in our war
against addictions is truly amazing! I began to
discover this on a personal level in the mid '90 while
'living on the streets' because of my addiction to
crack cocaine. There was a couple who would play
gospel music every week while serving a meal. The
fact that I am mentioning it now gives you an idea of
the impact that it had on me. To this very day, I, also,
look for the opportunity to play gospel music in
places where free meals are being served. I believe

that every Bible-based support group should provide gospel music as well.

First and foremost, I think that when we immerse ourselves in gospel music, then God recognizes that we really mean business. Whether we engage in music privately or publicly, we gain affirmation, we are motivated towards change, we receive encouragement, perhaps even insight. Music has the potential of relieving stress and easing sorrow. As we meditate on the words to various selections, we are given the ability to express our faith, our praise, our gratitude and love toward God. And then, most importantly, God is able to speak to us through such music!

Appendix G

Joy and rejoicing

Ex. 18:9 for all the goodness which the Lord had done
Lev. 23:40 before the Lord
Deut. 23:40 in all that you put your hand unto
Deut. 16:14 in thy feast
Deut. 26:11 in everything the Lord thy God hath given thee
1 Ki. 1:40 rejoiced with great joy
1 Chr. 16:10 let the heart of them rejoice that seek the Lord
Ps. 2:11 serve the Lord with fear and rejoice with trembling
Ps. 5:11 Let all that their trust in Thee rejoice
Ps. 9:14 Rejoice in Thy salvation
Ps. 21:1; 28:7 rejoice greatly
Ps. 68:3 exceedingly
Ps. 31:7 in Thy mercy
Ps. 32:11 ye righteous, ye upright in heart
Ps. 32:11 shout for joy
Ps. 85:6 a by-product of revival
Ps. 89:16 all the day
Ps. 90:14 through the satisfaction God gives
Ps. 90:14 all our days
Ps. 97:12 along with giving thanks
Ps. 98:4 singing
Ps. 105:3 glory in His holy name

Bibliography

Adams, Jay, *How to Help People Change* (Zondervan, 1986)
Adams, Jay, *Godliness through Discipline*
(P&R Publishing, 1972)
Baker, John, *Celebrate Recovery* (Zondervan, 2016)
Baker Theological Dictionary of the Bible
(Baker Academic, 2001)
Beale, G.K., *We Become What We Worship*
(InterVarsity Press, 2008)
Bridges, Jerry, *The Pursuit of Holiness*
(NavPress Publ. Group, 2010)
Bunyan, John, *Treatise on the Fear of God*
(free e-book at churhleaders.com, 1679)
Burns, Ralph O., *Basic Bible Truths*
(Regular Baptist Press, 1978)
Calvin, John, quotation
Chambers, Osward, *My Utmost for His Highest*
Taken from My Utmost for His Highest® by Oswald
Chambers, edited by James Reimann, © 1992 by Oswald
Chambers Publications Assn., Ltd., and used by permission
of Discovery House, Grand Rapids MI 49501. All rights
reserved. taken from My Utmost for His Highest® by
Oswald Chambers, edited by James Reimann, © 1992 by
Oswald Chambers Publications Assn., Ltd., and used by
permission of Discovery House, Grand Rapids MI
49501. All rights reserved.
Cleveland, Mike, *95 Theses for Pure Reformation*
(FOCUS PUB Incorporated, 2003)
Cleveland, Mike, *Pure Freedom: Breaking the Addiction to
Pornography* (Focus Pub. 2002)
Currington, Steve, *Recovery Through God's Truth*
(Reformers Unanimous, 2010)
Comiskey, Andrew, *Pursuing Sexual Wholeness* (Creation
House Strang Comm., 1989)

Delffs, Dudley J., A Repentant Heart (NavPress, 1995)
Dictionary.com
Eaton, Matthew G., *Eaton's Bible Dictionary* (CreateSpace Independent Publishing Platform, 2015)
Evans, Tony, *Fearing God* (video sermon series, The Urban Alternative)
Evans, Tony, *Returning to Your First Love (Moody Publishers, 2002)*
Funk and Wagnalls Standard Dictionary
Jackson, Tim, *When We Just Can't Stop*, Copyright 2011 by ODB Ministries, Grand Rapids, MI 49555. Used by permission. All rights reserved.
Keller, Timothy, *Counterfeit Gods* (Penguin, 2009)
Keller, Timothy, Shammas, Sam, New City Catechism (Crossway, 2017)
Lockyer, Herbert, *All the Divine Names and Titles in the Bible* (Zondervan, 1975)
MacArthur, John, *Hard to Believe* (2010, Thomas Nelson)
Mack, Wayne A., *The Distinguishing Feature of Christian Counseling* (article)
Manton, Thomas, *Exposition of the Epistle of James* (2001, Sovereign Grace Publisher's Inc)
Mason, Eric, <u>Manhood Restored</u> (Lifeway Press, 2015)
Meadors, Edward P., *Idolatry and the Hardening of the Heart* (T&T Clark, 2006)
Merriam-Webster's Dictionary
Narcotics Anonymous
Orville, Nave J., *Nave's Topical Bible* (Thomas Nelson, 1988)
Piper, John, *A Hunger for God* (Crossway Books, 1997)
Powlinson, David, *Idols of the Heart and "Vanity Fair"* (article)
Ryrie, Charles C., *The Ryrie Study Bible* ((Zondervan, 1986)
Shaw, Mark E., *The Heart of Addiction: A Biblical Perspective* (FOCUS Publishing, 2008)

Spurgeon, Charles H., quotation
Spurstowe, William, *The Wiles of Satan*
(CreateSpace Independent Pub. Platform, 2016)
Stanley, Charles, *The Blessings of Brokenness*
(Zondervan, 1997)
Thorndike-Barnhart Comprehensive Dictionary
Unger, Merrill F., Harrison, R.K., *New Unger's Bible
Dictionary* (Moody Publishers, 2006)
Vine's Expository Dictionary of Biblical Words
Watson, Thomas, *The Doctrine of Repentance* (Banner of
Truth Trust, 1668, 1987)
Webster's Dictionary
Welch, Edward T., *Addictions: A Banquet in the Grave*
(P&R Publishing, 2001)
Westminster Shorter Catechism (number 1)
The Valley of Vision, Man's Great End (Banner of Truth
Trust, 1975)

Index

Verses by Chapter

(all verses are KJV unless otherwise noted)
A "no" is an indication that the verse is referred to but not quoted. Appendixes verses not included.

Introduction
<u>Bible Versus Addictions</u>
2 Pet. 1:3
2 Tim. 3:16-17
Ps. 19:7-11
Rom. 15:4
1 Cor. 10:6
<u>Christ-centered answers</u>
Isa. 11:2-3a NIV
<u>Idolatry Assassination</u>
1 Thes. 1:9
Gen. 35:2 NAS
Josh. 24:14
Ps. 29:2 NIV
Rom. 10:10 NJKV

Chapter 1
Reasoning
Isa. 1:18a
Pro. 29:18
Psalm 139:23-24
<u>Before the Lord</u>
Isa. 59:1-2
<u>A frame of reverence</u>
Eccl. 12:13 NIV
Ja. 3:15 NIV
1 Sam. 2:30 no
Lev. 25:36 no
Deut. 6:24 no

Pro. 14:26 no
Ps. 25:13 no
Pro. 1:29
Jer. 44:10 no
Jer. 2:19 no
Zep. 3:8 no
Matt. 15:8 no
Jer. 3:8 no
Deut. 25:19 no
2 Ki. 17:35 no
Ps. 55:19 no
Pro. 10:27 no
Eccl. 8:13 no
Zep. 3:7 no

Chapter 2
The Reality of Addiction: Idolatry
Isa. 1:18
Conviction
Jn. 16:8 no
Ps. 51:4a
Spiritual implications
1 Jn. 5:21 Ampl. Version
Making sacrifices
Rom. 12:1
Dominated by an addiction
Ps. 104:4
Gen. 1:28 no
1 Jon 2:15 no
Matt. 22:37 no
Glory, honor and praise
Ps. 29:2
The idols in the Bible vs. the idols of today
2 Chron. 28:23 no
Marks of idolatry

Numerous references (see chapter)
What about you?
2 Cor. 7:10

Chapter 3
The Reality of Deceit
Scriptural proof
Gal. 5:19-21 no
Gal. 6:8 no
Ps. 16:4a
Isa. 42:17 NAS
Ps. 97:7
Isa. 28:15
Isa. 41:29
Isa. 44:20
Jer. 10:14
The high price of idolatry
1 Ki.9:6-9a Ampl. Version
Sold out
Ps. 106:39 no
An unequal exchange
Isa. 44:9-15, 20 Ampl. Version
The futility of idolatry
Pro. 21:17 no
Pro. 23:21 no
Pro. 20:1
How families are affected
Ps. 106:35-39
2 Ki. 17:17 NKJV
Master of deception
1 Pet. 5:8
2 Cor. 11:4 no
World of deception
2 Pet. 2:18-19 no
Isa. 5:20-21

166

Heart of deception
Eph. 4:22 no
Matt. 13:22 no
Heb. 3:13 no
Jer. 17:9 Ampl. Version
Ps. 139:23-24
Ps. 19:14
Pro. 4:23
Jn. 8:32

Chapter 4
The Real You
Rom. 12:3
Pro. 3:7
Isa. 53:6a
Pro. 14:12
Pro. 16:25
1 Jn. 5:11-13 no
A natural born fact
2 Tim. 3:1-4
1 Cor. 2:14
Gal. 5:19-20
Rom. 7:18
Sinful nature
Rom. 5:12
Giving in to the flesh
Lk. 9:23
Matt. 26:41
1 Ki. 3:7-10 no
Defilement
Mk. 7:21-23
Jer. 17:9-10 no
Matt. 26:31-35 no
Matt. 26:69-75 no
On your own

Lk. 21:34
An underlying factor
1 Pet. 2:11
1 Thes. 5:19 no
Eph. 4:18 no
Eph. 2:3 no
Jn. 5:40 no
Beyond our own nature
Acts 4:12
Lk. 15:16 no
Jn. 10:10
Deut 30:19-20
Jn. 14:6 no
Christ alone
Rom. 8:8 no
Rom. 5:1 no
Heb. 11:6
Matt. 5:20
2 Cor. 5:21

Chapter 5
Definition and dynamics of repentance
Conviction and repentance
Ps. 32:8-9
The process of repentance
2 cor. 7:11
Gen. 4:6-7
An attitude of brokenness
Ps. 51:17
Isa. 57:15
A summary of repentance
2 Pet. 3:9 no
2 Tim. 2:24-25 no
Rev. 3:18-19 no

Chapter 6
Acts of repentance
Making a clean break
Josh. 24:15 NAS
1 Kin. 18:21
Jn. 6:66-69 Ampl. Version
Matt. 6:24 Ampl. Version
Acts 19:18-19
2 Cor. 10:5

Temptation
Acts 4:12
Col. 2:3 no
Pro. 11:14
Eccl. 12:11
Heb. 4:15-16
Ps. 61:2
2 Cor. 10:4-5
Fasting
Jon. 3:3-8
(advantages)
Lk. 20:34
Heb. 5:8
1 Jn. 2:28
Communion
(fellowship with God)
Jn. 1:1
Heb. 1:1-2a
2 Pet. 1:3-4
Rom. 12:2a
 (fellowship with others)
Jn. 6:63

Chapter 7
Rejoicing in the Lord
Acts 3:19
Neh. 8:10
Fellowship with God
1 Jn. 1:3-4
Practice
Gal. 5:22 no
1 Pet. 1:8
The fruit of the Spirit/supernatural
2 Cor. 7:4
Delight- multiple verses (see chapter)

Conclusion
Reason
Pro. 14:12
Repent
Isa. 55:7-9
2 Cor. 7:11 no
Jude 23 no
Matt. 22:37-39 no
Rejoice
Gal. 5:22 no
1 Cor. 2:9
Deut. 30:20
1 Jn. 4:19

Appendix A
Select verses on understanding
  1. God's
  2. Lacking
  3. Sought after
  4. Source
  5. Results

170

Appendix B
What is sobriety?
Matt. 6:33 no
Eccl. 12:13
Clean and Sober for the Right Reasons
1 Cor. 1:24 no
Phil. 2:12b
Ja. 3:13-17
Matt. 10:37-39
Ps. 86:11 no

Appendix C
The Idols in the Bible vs. the Idols of Today
2 Chron. 28:23 no
Deut. 32:15-29 no
Ps. 32:9a
Select passages on idolatry
Warnings against idolatry
God's judgment against idolatry
Futility and deceit of idolatry
Examples of idolatry
Repentance: Turning from idolatry

Appendix D
Essential Reverence
Pro. 9:10 no
1 Cor. 1:24 no
Select passages on reverence
The basis of our reverence
Characteristics/Components
Commanded
Refusal
Examples
Proof
Rewards

Is it Spiritual?
2 Tim. 2:5 no
2 Cor. 5:15

Appendix E
Actions
Select words on repentance out the scriptures no
The Importance of Using Various Resources
Pro. 2:1-4
Pro. 11:14
Acts 20:27 no
Acts 20:20 no
1 Cor. 12:21 no

Appendix F
Support groups
Acts 20:20a
Pro. 29:18 no
2 Tim. 1:7
Starting a group of your own
Matt. 9:36
Pro. 24:11
Format
Scripture reading
1Pet. 2:11
2 Cor. 5:15
Rom. 13:11-14
1 Jn. 2:28-29

Appendix G
Joy and rejoicing
Select phrases

Thanks for reading! If you enjoyed this book or found it useful, I'd be very grateful if you'd post a short review on Amazon. Your support really does make a difference and I read all the reviews personally so I can get your feedback and make this book even better.

(Note: For further readings please visit one or all the following:)

www.turningtogodfromidols.com

www.facebook.com/sobrietyinChrist/

www.facebook.com/turningtoGodfromidols/

www.facebook.com/aweinawe/

Free online study at https://bible-verses-addictions.learnnn.com/tgfi

Books by Gregory Madison include:
Turning to God from Idols
Sobriety for Christmas
The Basics of Turning to God from Idols
Bible Verses Addictions- The Problem, Volumes 1&2
Bible Verses Addictions- Solution, Volumes 1& 2

Made in the USA
San Bernardino, CA
16 February 2019